Assisting Examination Ca
The Study of *Othe*

The notes that follow are primarily to understanding the complexities of *Othello* in order to write knowledgeable essays for examination purposes. I wrote them to aid my students, who found them most accessible and useful.

I am not a Shakespearean scholar, just a highly qualified teacher with years of experience, who wishes, not only to encourage young people to ponder The Bard's characters, themes, imagery and techniques, but also seriously consider the questions raised in his play, many still significant in the world today.

Warm wishes and good luck studying *Othello*.

A E Chambers

Assisting Examination Candidates in
The Study of *Othello*

by A E Chambers
Copyright 2016 A E Chambers

A E Chambers has asserted her rights under the Copyright, Designs and Patents Act 1988 to be identified as the author of this work.

This book is sold subject to the condition that it shall not, by way of trade or otherwise be lent, resold, hired out, or otherwise be circulated without the author's prior consent in any form of binding or cover other than that in which it is published and without a similar condition, including this condition, being imposed on the subsequent purchaser.

Thank you for respecting the hard work of this author.

Website: aechambersnovelist.com

Facebook: Amelia Chambers

Twitter: aechambersnove1

Email: aechambersnovelist@gmail.com

Contents

A Short Biography of William Shakespeare

Section One: Characters
1.1 Othello
1.2 Iago
1.3 Desdemona
1.4 Michael Cassio
1.5 Roderigo
1.6 Emilia
1.7 Brabantio
1.8 Bianca
1.9 Lodovico
1.10 The Duke of Venice
1.11 Montano
1.12 Gratiano

Section Two: Themes
2.1 The Theme of Jealousy
2.2 The Theme of Emotion versus Reason
2.3 The Theme of Appearance versus Reality
2.4 The Theme of Deception, Deceit and Betrayal
2.5 The Theme of Love and Duty
2.6 The Theme of Prejudice
2.7 The Theme of Punishment, Justice and Retribution

Section Three: Imagery
3.1 Images of Light and Dark
3.2 Images of Sight and Blindness
3.3 Images of Disease and Corruption
3.4 Images of Clothing
3.5 Images of Food, Appetite and Hunger
3.6 Images of Heaven, Hell, Demons, Monsters, Fate and Fortune
3.7 Natural Imagery
3.8 Images of Magic and Witchcraft
3.9 The Handkerchief

Section Four: Soliloquies
4.1 Introduction to Iago's Soliloquies
4.2 Iago's First Soliloquy
4.3 Iago's Second Soliloquy
4.4 Iago's Third Soliloquy
4.5 Iago's Fourth Soliloquy
4.6 Iago's Fifth Soliloquy
4.7 Othello's Soliloquy

Section Five: Techniques
5.1 Dramatic Devices
5.2 Music
5.3 Literary Devices
5.4 Rhyme and Prose
5.5 Irony
5.6 Settings

Section Six: Essay Plans
6.1 Introduction to Essay Plans
6.2 Plan for an essay on Fear and Pity in *Othello*
6.3 Plan for an essay on Drama and Intrigue in *Othello*
6.4 Plan for an essay on The Minor Characters in *Othello*
6.5 Plan for an essay on "It is the evil that enthrals the audience in *Othello*, not the good."
6.6 Plan for an essay on "Othello's foolishness rather than Iago's cleverness lead to tragedy in Shakespeare's *Othello*."
6.7. Plan for an essay on "Desdemona is just too good to be true."
6.8 Plan for an essay on Why Study *Othello* in the 21st Century?
6.9 Plan for an essay on Why do the characters trust each other?
6.10 Plan for an essay on The Treatment of Women in *Othello*.
6.11 Plan for an essay on Imagery in *Othello*
6.12 Plan for an essay on "Shakespeare's play demonstrates the weakness of human judgement."
6.13 Plan for an essay on "Othello is a character with whom the audience can sympathise."
6.14 Plan for an essay on Dramatic Scene(s) in *Othello*

6.15 Plan for an essay on "Iago is an insidious villain with whom the audience has no sympathy."

6.16 Plan for an essay on Shakespeare is a poet and playwright of great renown. How is this proved in the play *Othello*?

A Short Biography of William Shakespeare

William Shakespeare was born in Stratford upon Avon, England, in 1564, the third of eight children. His birthday is usually celebrated on April 23rd to coincide with St George's Day, although his actual date of birth is unknown. His father was a successful glove maker, commodities merchant and alderman.

Shakespeare attended Kings New School, where he studied rhetoric, Latin and the Classics, but he left at the age of fifteen, the required age at the time, or possibly because of his father's financial difficulties.

At the age of 18 he married Anne Hathaway, a woman of 26. Six months later, she gave birth to Susanna. Twins, Judith and Hamnet, were born two years after their older sister. Sadly Hamnet died at the age of 11, but Shakespeare's career went from strength to strength.

He appeared on the London theatre scene in 1592 and, when plague closed the theatres, it is believed he wrote his sonnets and poem, *Venus and Adonis*. In 1594 he became a member of the Lord Chamberlain's Men, a theatre company he co-owned, but he continued to act and, of course, write, appearing before Queen Elizabeth I, who favoured his plays. It was her successor, James I, who bestowed his blessing and the company's name was changed to the King's Men.

Shakespeare was a very astute businessman who invested in property and by 1600 he was the co-owner of the Globe Theatre and a theatre in Blackfriars, both in London, as well as the second biggest house in his hometown. The Globe burned down, but was reconstructed in the 1980s, attracting actors and actresses from all over the world to take on challenging roles to thrill contemporary audiences.

Shakespeare died in 1616 and his work was published by former friends and colleagues. The plays are divided into tragedies, histories and comedies and are not considered original, nor historically accurate. No scripts written in Shakespeare's hand have ever been found, leading to much speculation about The Bard's actual participation in their writing, but they are still incredibly popular, as they are an insight into the passions and proclivities of the human race.

Section One: Characters

Section 1.1: Othello

The Moor, Othello, is a dark skinned man, who has attained the rank of officer in the Venetian army. He has several fatal failings: jealousy, gullibility and self-denigration, thereby becoming an easy mark for the master plotter, Iago.

In the first act Othello is derogatorily described by Iago, via animal imagery, as an

> "old black ram ... a Barbary horse",

implying he is of middle age and from the north of Africa (the Barbary Coast). Although the term *"Barbary"* could easily be a play on words for the more insulting term, 'barbarian', a man who is not as civilised as the Venetians. Iago is disparaging the man, whom he hates, in an effort to enrage Brabantio.

The audience quickly learns Othello is far from barbaric. He is an eloquent speaker seen when he reveals why Desdemona fell in love with him and he with her.

> "I will a round unvarnished tale deliver.
> Of my whole course of love",

he begins, then tells the duke and Brabantio,

> "She loved me for the dangers that I pass'd,
> And I loved her, that she did pity them."

His eloquence is also manifested in the final scene when he touchingly explains how he wishes to be remembered before he falls on his sword.

> "Speak of me as I am. Nothing extenuate. Not set down
> aught in malice. Then you must speak
> Of one who lov'd not wisely, but too well ...

*Of one whose hand
(Like the base Indian) threw a pearl away
Richer than all his tribe"*.

Despite his eloquence, note how he belittles himself comparing himself, via a simile, to a *"base Indian"*. He does the same at the beginning of the play when he tells the Duke,

*"Rude am I in my speech,
And little blessed with the soft phrase of peace"*.

Othello has a tendency to denigrate himself, which is in stark contrast to his physical strength and prowess. It is this self-depreciation Iago plays upon. If Othello had a little more self-confidence and self-belief, Iago may have found the Moor a little more difficult to dupe.

Othello is a man who stands apart from the other characters, both physically and metaphorically. He is the last to arrive in Cyprus, following the battle with the Turk. He stays in the shadows when Cassio and Iago talk, supposedly, about Desdemona. His *"epilepsy"* and exotic past also set him apart from others. Othello is repeatedly conveyed as an outsider and he does little to combat this.

Yet, Othello is a highly praised warrior. Cassio informs the Moor he has been sent by the senate

"about three several quests to search you out",

evoking the soldier is in much demand by the leaders of Venice. He is sent to battle against the Turk and, being successful, his reward is to become the political leader of Cyprus. To his credit Othello, at the end of the play, reminds all present he has

"done the state some service"

and should be remembered as such, rather than for his misdeeds.

Sadly, Othello is a poor judge of character. Considering he has known his *"ancient",* Iago, for some time he seems to have no idea of the man's hatred of him. Othello's jealousy blinds him to Iago's machinations and he's gullible believing him to be *"honest"*. It is ironic he cannot see the evil lurking within the ranks he leads, despite his travels and experience.

Similarly, Othello seems to know little about Emilia, or of Cassio, apparently unaware the man has

"little brains for drinking"

and is not a habitual drunk. He even has doubts about Desdemona, but is this exacerbated by his love for her and his fatal jealousy? Initially he tells Iago,

"Exchange me for a goat
When I shall turn the business of my soul
To such exsufflicate, and blown surmises",

referring to suspicions of Desdemona's unfaithfulness. Yet, Iago sprinkles doubt about Desdemona's fidelity causing the Moor to wonder,

"Why did I marry?'

and he makes the fateful decision to observe his wife and asks Emilia to do the same. Consider this: had Othello a better insight into the people around him, would he have been as gullible?

The theme of emotion versus reason is very apparent in the character, Othello. He loses all reason when he becomes obsessively jealous. He is led to believe Desdemona is having an affair with Cassio, when Iago tells him,

"In sleep I heard him say, sweet Desdemona
Let us be wary, let us hide our loves"

and Iago embellishes the lie, stating Cassio, would

> *"wring my hand ... then kiss me hard"*.

Othello's rage comes to the fore when Iago concludes the falsehood, stating he had seen

> *"Cassio wipe his beard"*

with the *"handkerchief"* Othello had given his wife as a present. In his defence he is skilfully manipulated by Iago, who puts him in a rage so strong, the Moor has an epileptic fit, a symptom of his emotional turmoil.

The tragedy is Othello's jealousy overrides his reason. He refuses to listen to his wife and, enraged, he kills her, only to find out the dreadful truth about the handkerchief and his wife's fidelity from Emilia. When she realises her husband's treachery, she accuses Iago,

> *"You told a lie, an odious damn lie ... a wicked lie."*

In a moment of remorse Othello does, what he believes to be, the honourable thing: he takes his own life.

It is because Othello loves Desdemona that Iago is able to orchestrate his plot. The marriage is not arranged, like many during the Renaissance, but almost a fairy story, with the young Desdemona, seduced and enamoured by a dashing, exotic, worldly man. Othello views his winning of the fair lady as *"wondrous"*, but Brabantio suspects Othello has weaved a spell on his daughter, who has seen past the colour of the Moor's *"sooty bosom"* and married him.

The handkerchief supposedly has

> *"magic in the web of it"*,

as it was made by a *"sibyl"* and the silkworms, providing the silk, were *"hallowed"*. Yet the only *"magic"* Othello has employed to woo Desdemona is his narration of epic tales, resulting in true love. The audience is left in no doubt Desdemona reciprocates Othello's love for her, thus their demise is more poignant.

Othello is a man who is betrayed by his friend who he expected to be loyal. He is

"led by the nose, as asses are"

and, although a physically capable warrior, his jealousy, lack of judgement and credulity lead him to madness and eventual destruction.

Section 1.2: Iago

Iago is possibly one of the most heinous villains in all of Shakespeare's plays. His insidious actions, fuelled by revenge and anger, are set on destroying Othello. His ability to manipulate those around him, twist an argument to his favour and hide his true intent make him one of the more compelling characters in the play. It is very easy to love to hate Iago.

Early in the play Iago admits several times,

> "I hate the Moor"

but his reasons for such an emotional declaration do not equate with the deep hatred he harbours. Does this make him a more despicable villain?

He believes Othello may have slept with his wife.

> "It is thought abroad that 'twixt my sheets
> He has done my office",

he states and he wishes to get even with Othello. His revenge being similar to Biblical vengeance in Exodus 20: an eye for an eye, Iago will take *"wife for wife"*. But he has no real proof of his wife's adultery.

Furthermore, Iago is enraged because he has not been promoted and, to add insult to injury, Othello has chosen Cassio to be his lieutenant, a man with less experience. But do these reasons lack conviction for the man's all-consuming hatred?

His desire to avenge the Moor is overwhelming and he has no qualms employing his wife, Emilia, manipulating Rodrigo and abusing Desdemona, to achieve his goal. He even seems to luxuriate in his cunning admitting,

> "I am not what I am."

and fully explains he will put on the appearance of a *"knee-crooking knave"* and be *"obsequious"* to his master. Does his pretence and wanton disregard for others make Iago even more egregious?

Iago is insightful and intelligent, which makes him a dangerous villain, but one the audience can almost admire. Certainly his manipulation of the gullible Roderigo may be viewed as humorous and it is difficult to sympathise with the foolish Venetian who gives Iago money, firmly believing he is likely to win the fair hand of Desdemona, despite her marriage to the Moor. Iago is capable of seeing a man's flaws and uses them to his advantage. He certainly recognises Othello's.

> *"The green ey'd monster"*

is Othello's hamartia and Iago uses this knowledge to put the Moor

> *"into a jealousy so strong
> That judgement cannot cure."*

It is fascinating to watch Iago weave his *"web"*, ensuring Othello overhears a conversation regarding Cassio's relationship with Bianca, which Othello misinterprets, thinking the discussion concerns his wife's dalliance with the lieutenant.

Furthermore, Iago employs his wife to steal the handkerchief, the first gift Othello gave Desdemona, which Cassio finds in his room and gives to Bianca. When Othello sees Cassio proffer the present, his desire for the lieutenant's demise is complete.

It is because Iago is fully aware of a person's weaknesses he can machinate events to his advantage. Aware Cassio has

> *"little brains for drinking"*

Iago easily makes the innocent man drunk, ensuring a fight ensues, resulting in Cassio's demotion. Iago then suggests Desdemona could speak to her husband on Cassio's behalf. Knowing Desdemona's tendency to pity others, after all isn't that why she fell in love with the Moor, Iago can presume she will do as Cassio asks. Iago knows Othello, who loves his wife deeply, will do anything for her.

Can Iago be admired in the manner he uses his knowledge and intelligence to bring about the ruin of Othello and Cassio? Consider what Iago could have achieved had he put his plotting ability to better use.

Iago's intelligence comes to the fore again when he is able to argue both sides of a contention. Consider what he says about *"reputation"* to Cassio and later, states the exact opposite to Othello.

He tells Cassio,

> *"Reputation is an idle and most false imposition, oft got without merit and lost without deserving."*

To Othello he claims,

> *"good name in man and woman, dear my lord is the immediate jewel of their soul."*

Shakespeare subtly puts forward that reputation can equally be false and worthy.

This is also a good example of Iago's ability to act. He has built up his own reputation of being *"honest"* and Othello has made the man his *"ancient"* (captain) based on this. Did Iago manifest this reputation in the same way he has created a *"web"* of deceit around Othello?

The one time Iago is *"honest"* is during his soliloquies. The audience is well aware of his plotting and intent, creating a palpable tension as his machinations come to pass. Unlike the characters, the audience is aware of his dual personality and knows when he is being deceitful.

Is his marriage to Emilia equally ambiguous? Does he love his wife, or does his status as a married man make him appear more trustworthy? In fact, Iago shows an underlying contempt for women. He tells Roderigo,

"I would drown myself for the love of a guinea hen, I would change my humanity with a baboon",

implying he would not drown himself, nor be love-sick over a woman, but prefer to be a monkey!

Later he is most insulting of women accusing them of being duplicitous.

"You are pictures out of door, belles in your parlours; wildcats in your kitchens; saints in your injuries: devils being offended: players in your housewifery and housewives in your beds."

In the final act he shows no hesitation in telling his wife to *"hold your peace"* before killing her. She has become a threat and has to be silenced.

Iago abuses Desdemona, persuading Othello she has been unfaithful, by saying,

"She did deceive her father, marrying you".

He slyly echoes Brabantio's earlier warning, suggesting as Desdemona betrayed her father she could very well betray Othello. Iago's disparagement of women, denigrating them to sexual playthings and viewing them as *"sport"*, is sexist and is one reason some have put forward the notion he harbours a homosexual attraction to Othello. He often states his love for Othello and does his best to stop Othello from enjoying time with his new bride, but in soliloquy he claims he hates the man.

Iago is not a stereotypical villain the audience would expect. He lacks a conscience thus becoming amoral rather than immoral. Today he would be considered a psychopath who seeks power and has to be in control. He shows no remorse when those around him realise his deceit and he does not hesitate to kill Roderigo and Emilia in an attempt to hide his evil actions. His lack of conscience allows him to congratulate himself on his mastery in plotting the downfall of Cassio and the Moor. In soliloquy he relishes his achievements.

"The Moor already changes with my poison",

he gloats, making him a more fiendish villain.

Finally, Iago's absolute fate is undecided. It is left to Cassio to decide

"the time, the place, the torture"

of the man who has caused much *"anguish"*. As Lodovico says, the scene of three dead bodies *"poisons sight"*. Directors have used this to their advantage. In Orson Welles' 1952 production, Iago is encaged and hauled up above the castle walls, left to starve and feed the crows. The theme of justice is therefore brought to the fore. What punishment would you bestow on Iago?

Section 1.3: Desdemona

Desdemona is a beautiful Venetian woman, much loved by her father, Brabantio, adored by Roderigo and revered by her husband, Othello. She shuns convention by marrying an outsider, a dark skinned Moor, rather than a rich, Venetian gentleman and the first the audience hears of Desdemona is derogatory. She is the *"white ewe"* being tupped by the *"black ram"*, highlighting her break from the status quo. The fact she has married without her father's knowledge and consent also shows how she has forsaken her filial duty.

She initially brings to the fore the conundrum as to whom a married woman should be loyal, her parents or her husband. The Fifth Commandment in the Bible states 'Honour thy father and thy mother.' Yet her marriage vow insists she 'love, honour and obey' her husband. Which is more important: her filial duty to Brabantio or her spousal duty to Othello? Desdemona voices the dilemma.

> *"I do perceive here a divided duty.*
> *To you I am bound for life and education...*
> *But here's my husband*
> *And so much duty, as my mother show'd*
> *To you; preferring you before her father."*

Desdemona respects her parents enough to emulate her mother by putting spousal duty above filial duty.

It is made perfectly clear Desdemona's love for Othello is based on him being exotic, a dangerous adventurer, a man who has survived

> *"disastrous chances ... moving accidents in floods and field...hair-breadth 'scapes"*,

captured and *"sold to slavery"*.

Even the duke can understand why she is attracted to the Moor.

> "I think this tale would win my daughter too",

he says, underlying a notion many women find men of action more appealing than those less worldly.

Arguably Desdemona is not a weak and demure woman, but one who shows an independent streak, an authority and an intelligence, especially when speaking to her father. She insists on accompanying her new husband to Cyprus asking the duke,

> "Let me go with him."

Once in Cyprus she is in charge of Othello's household, acts as his hostess and reveals a quick wittedness when she bandies with Iago in Act II Scene I. The scene, filled with sexual innuendo, also reflects Desdemona's sensuality and recent nuptials.

To her detriment, Desdemona's independent spirit allows her to stand up for Cassio, asking her husband outright,

> "If I have any grace or power to move you,
> His present reconciliation take".

She is aware she has to show loyalty and obedience to her husband, which conflicts with her sense of injustice and she pushes for Othello to hear her.

> "Why then, tomorrow night, or Tuesday morn...
> In faith he is penitent."

This strong sense of injustice manifests itself once again after Othello strikes her.

> "I have not deserved this"

she tells him, but, as the play progresses, Desdemona appears torn between being an obedient wife and an independent woman.

There are times when she is submissive, especially when she takes the blame for her own murder. Emilia asks,

> *"Who has done this deed?"*

Desdemona enigmatically replies,

> *"Nobody, I myself. Farewell.*
> *Commend me to my kind lord. O, farewell".*

Why does she not lay the blame on Othello? Is it because she loves him? Is it because she feels she has failed him? Or is it because she wishes to retain some independence, even on her deathbed? It may be said the suffocation of Desdemona with a pillow can be construed as symbolic of man's desire to stifle the independence of women. To literally stop their mouths from voicing independent thought. Does Desdemona become less independent and more obedient to her husband under the constraints of marriage?

Her forgiveness of her husband may lend a clue to Desdemona's feelings, as she has been unable to prevent her husband's jealousy and decline into madness. She sings a song before she dies mirroring her own situation.

> *"She was in love; and he proved mad*
> *And did forsake her. She had a song of willow...*
> *And she died singing it."*

Shakespeare's portrayal of Desdemona is complex as, beneath her outward beauty, she is an intelligent, good-humoured person in her own right. Via this character he raises the interesting question of women, once they have fallen in love and marry: Do they lose their autonomy?

Section 1.4: Michael Cassio

Cassio is a young and inexperienced soldier in the Venetian army, who is promoted to lieutenant much to Iago's chagrin. Iago claims Cassio is an *"arithmetician"*, a scholar, who has little experience of battle. He has

*"never set a squadron in the field
Nor the division of a battle knows."*

Iago's jealousy and anger ensures Cassio becomes a victim in his *"web"* of lies and deceit. The lieutenant loses his *"reputation"*, whilst the Moor is destroyed.

Totally unaware and naive, Cassio does not see the manipulative, deceitful nature of others and is completely unaware of Iago's machinations. The handsome soldier admits he has

"poor and unhappy brains for drinking"

giving Iago the knowledge that alcohol could be his fatal flaw. Indeed, plied with alcohol by a fawning Iago, Cassio loses his reason when drunk. Subsequently he is demoted following an orchestrated brawl, conducted by Iago, who reaps the rewards of his insidious actions by being promoted in the young man's stead.

Loyal to Othello, Cassio is extremely ashamed of his behaviour and frets over the loss of his *"reputation"*, believing a man without regard is no more than an animal.

"Oh, I have lost my reputation! I have lost the immortal part of myself, and what remains is bestial."

The masterful Iago uses Cassio's naiveté, good looks and friendship with Desdemona to great effect, suggesting the lieutenant should ask Desdemona to speak for him and plead his case for reinstatement.

> *"I do beseech you ...*
> *I may again exist and be a member of his love*
> *Whom I with all the office of my heart*
> *Entirely honour."*

Unbeknownst to Cassio, Iago tells the Moor, Desdemona is having an adulterous affair with the young lieutenant and Othello believes he has proof of his wife's affair when he overhears a conversation between Desdemona and Lodovico.

> *"Lodovico: Is there division 'twixt my lord and Cassio?*
> *"Desdemona: A most unhappy one; I would do much*
> *T'atone them, for the love I bear to Cassio."*

Iago is fully cognisant of Cassio's love of women as he speaks openly to Desdemona, Bianca and he kisses Emilia, much to Iago's annoyance. Cassio is charismatic and Bianca, unfortunately falls under his charm. He refers to her as *"sweet Bianca"* and gives her the *"handkerchief"* he found asking her to make a copy.

To his detriment, like Iago, Cassio has a low opinion of women, classifying them as either virtuous or whores. He views Desdemona as

> *"a maid that paragons description and wild fame"*.

But he toys with Bianca, using a double negative to express his ambiguous feelings,

> *"Not that I love you not"*,

later dismissing the woman, because she is a prostitute.

> *"I marry her! What? A customer! Prithee, bear some*
> *charity to my wit"*,

he scoffs, then later complains to Iago that the woman is too demanding.

> *"She haunts me in every place ... So hangs and lolls and weeps upon me."*

Othello, overhearing this conversation, tragically believes Cassio is talking about Desdemona.

In the final scene Cassio is the only one left alive who has been manipulated by *"honest"* Iago.

Lodovico tells those present,

> *"Cassio rules in Cyprus",*

and he is left to decide Iago's punishment.

> *"To you, lord governor,*
> *Remains the censure of this hellish villain*
> *The time, the place, the torture."*

The audience is left to wonder what Cassio will do and if such a decision should be put on the shoulders of such a young, inexperienced man.

Section 1.5: Roderigo

A gullible, Venetian gentleman, Roderigo, is besotted with Desdemona and jealous of the Moor, making him an easy mark for the manipulative Iago. He is a man whose emotions cloud his reason, yet letters found in his pocket prove the ancient's villainy.

Foolishly, Roderigo believes money will buy Desdemona's hand in marriage and he puts his trust in the insidious Iago. It is later in the play when the audience learns Roderigo's fortune has been spent on a futile quest to woo Desdemona, his money having been secretly *"bobbed"* (purloined) by Iago.

His jealousy and disgust with the Moor, having married the woman of his dreams, clouds his reason. He believes Iago's lies and under Iago's instruction, views Cassio as a threat to his pursuit of Desdemona, goading the lieutenant to fight when he is drunk. Even when Roderigo suspects Iago is using him he continues to do the ancient's bidding. He says,

"Everyday thou daff'st me with some device Iago",

but he agrees to kill Cassio despite thinking,

"I have no great devotion to the deed".

The old adage 'love is blind' applies to Roderigo, but some would argue he is deaf and dumb as well!

As Iago's *"web"* unravels at speed, Roderigo is stabbed by the evil Iago, but he has outwitted the master plotter by writing letters telling of Iago's schemes. The *"papers"*, found in the dead Roderigo's pocket, prove to be Iago's undoing, when read by Lodovico.

*"The one of them imports
the death of Cassio to be undertook by Roderigo ...*

> *And this, it seems, Roderigo meant to t'have sent this damn'd villain,*
> *But that belike, Iago in the nick*
> *Came in and satisfied him."*

Roderigo, it appears, had written to Iago complaining of his actions, but Iago, pretending to be his friend, killed him first.

Roderigo is a counterpart to Cassio, both used by Iago to orchestrate the demise of Othello, both young and naive, unaware of the evilness around them. Both lose their reason, Cassio via drink, Roderigo through his love for the *"fair maid"*, and both lose their status: Roderigo his *"fortune"*, Cassio his *"reputation"* and his rank. Roderigo is ultimately killed, whereas Cassio lives to decide the fate of Roderigo's murderer.

Roderigo is a foolish, gullible, love-struck man, but is redeemed somewhat in the *"papers"* found after his assassination.

Section 1.6: Emilia

Iago's wife and Desdemona's maid, Emilia, finds herself in the unenviable position of being torn between her marriage vow, to 'love, honour and obey her husband' and Christ's Second Commandment: 'Love they neighbour as thyself'; her love or loyalty being to Desdemona.

She is used by her husband to purloin the handkerchief which will implicate Cassio. She admits

> *"What he will do with it,*
> *Heaven knows, not I",*

and questions Iago, but to no avail. Nevertheless, she does her spousal duty, which she denounces at the end of the play. Deciding a loyalty to Desdemona trumps her husband's lies and deceit, she reveals Iago to be a despicable villain.

> *"Your reports have set the murder on ... villainy, villainy, villainy',*

she blames Iago and reveals how she was asked to *"steal"* the handkerchief.

> *"I found it*
> *And I did give it to my husband",*

she explains. Iago slays in order to silence her.

Emilia seems older than Desdemona because she has a more worldly wisdom. In the same way Iago has a low opinion of women, his wife has an unfavourable view of men. She actually blames them for setting a bad example for women, saying,

> *"The ills we do, their ills instruct us so."*

She claims that if men ill-treat their women, then like men, they will want their *"revenge"*.

She propounds a theory that there is little difference between men and women.

> *"Let husbands know*
> *Their wives have sense like them: they see and smell*
> *And have their palates both for sweet and sour..."*

She even claims women have the same sexual appetites as men, *"desires for sport"* and the same *"frailties"*. It is a speech reminiscent of Shylock's in *The Merchant of Venice* when he points out the similarities between Christians and Jews.

Her views hint that men are idiotic, evil and depraved and Shakespeare does little to prove her wrong. Rodcrigo is certainly foolish, her husband depraved and evil, Othello and Cassio lacking judgement of their fellow men.

Thus Emilia becomes a strong voice for the prejudice shown towards women. She does her spousal duty but, like her mistress, she has a strong sense of justice and speaks out against her husband's *"villainy"*, paying for her honesty with her life.

Section 1.7: Brabantio

Brabantio highlights two main aspects of the play. Firstly his overprotectiveness of his daughter means Desdemona is torn between a duty to her father and a duty to her husband; a recurring theme in Shakespeare's plays. A woman in the Renaissance had to choose between the fifth Commandment, of loving a parent, and the marriage vow, of obeying and honouring a husband. Secondly, Brabantio highlights the theme of racism, seeing the marriage between his white daughter and a man of *"sooty"* complexion to be *"unnatural"*.

Brabantio's overprotectiveness of Desdemona is seen when he tells Roderigo,

"I have charged thee not to haunt about my doors:
In honest plainness thou hast heard me say
My daughter is not for thee".

Iago is fully aware of the love Brabantio has for his daughter and uses this knowledge to enrage the father, suspecting he will do his best to dissolve the marriage.

Iago is most insulting of the relationship between the Venetian woman and the Moor. By employing animal imagery Iago tells Brabantio,

"An old black ram is tupping your white ewe."

Like Othello and Cassio, Brabantio is unaware he is being manipulated by Iago.

Brabantio has difficulty coming to terms with the fact his daughter is old enough to be married and, not wanting to blame his daughter of eloping with the Moor, accuses Othello of being a thief and abusing *"her delicate youth"*. The enraged father is then quick to claim the exotic man has cast a spell or some *"charm"* of *"magic"* over his daughter, so desperate is he to find some explanation for Desdemona's actions. He asks Roderigo,

> "Is there not charms
> By which the property of youth and maidhood
> May be abused? Have you not read, Roderigo,
> Of some such thing?"

His preoccupation with the use of witchcraft is thwarted by Desdemona, who explains she loves Othello and does not want to be parted from him. She convinces the Court Othello has employed no magic, which upsets Brabantio further. He tells her,

> "For your sake, jewel,
> I am glad at soul I have no other child:
> For thy escape would teach me tyranny,
> To hang clogs on them."

The metaphor, *"jewel"*, reveals Brabantio sees his daughter as a possession, but his tone is bitter, relieved he will experience the pain of a daughter's betrayal only once.

Although no man seems good enough for Desdemona in the eyes of her father, Brabantio is most disparaging about Othello, showing a racial bias against the man, employing subtle animal imagery. He sees the marriage as

> "against the rules of nature"

and implies it is uncivilised.

> "This is Venice, my house is not a grange",

he scorns, meaning his abode is refined, not a farm where animals and baser behaviour reside.

He cannot believe his daughter fell

> "in love with what she feared to look on"

implying Othello is fearsome, even ugly.

> "She is abused, stol'n from me and corrupted,"

he claims, proving he sees Othello as a villain and inferior. Is Brabantio concerned for his daughter or for his own reputation in the Court?

He views Desdemona's choice of husband and wish to go with him to Cyprus as a betrayal and warns the Moor,

> "She has deceived her father; and may thee."

Via Brabantio, Shakespeare emotes discrimination present in the Court (as well as in today's world). He brings to the fore filial duty and evokes a father's desire for his daughter to remain a child or possession, rather than a woman in her own right.

Section 1.8: Bianca

The young woman, Bianca, is a courtesan, or prostitute, thus a woman of low rank. She is used, or more pertinently abused, by Cassio and Iago. Her presence proves men can have a low opinion of women.

Cassio visits Bianca and gives her the *"handkerchief"* he has found in his rooms and asks her to copy it. It is not, therefore, a romantic gift. He looks forward to his sexual dalliances with her, but is disdainful of marrying her, believing she is beneath him.

> *"Marry her! What? A customer? Prithee bear some charity to my wit."*

he tells Iago and laughs heartily at the idea.

Her relationship with Cassio is used by Iago to mislead Othello. A conversation discussing Cassio's feelings for Bianca is overheard by the Moor, who believes Cassio is speaking of his adultery with Desdemona. Cassio complains,

> *"She haunts me every place ... she falls about my neck."*

and Othello's jealous fury is inflamed.

Later Iago tries to shift the blame of Cassio's wounding onto the innocent woman by saying,

> *"Gentleman all, I do suspect this trash to be a party in this injury."*

Sadly, Bianca fulfils Emilia's belief that women are merely *"food"* to appease men's *"appetites"*.

Section 1.9: Lodovico

One of Brabantio's kinsmen, Lodovico, acts as a messenger from Venice to Cyprus. He is an honourable man, intent of doing his duty, delivering letters requiring Othello return to Venice and Cassio be governor.

Lodovico arrives in Cyprus to hear of a breach between Othello and Cassio, then to his dismay, witnesses Othello *"strike his wife"*. He reminds the Moor,

> *"This would not be believed in Venice",*

suggesting Othello is being uncivilised and demands he *"make her amends"*.

He is shocked by the change in the Moor questioning Iago,

> *"Are his wits safe? Is he not light of brain?"*

He is intelligent enough to realise there is turmoil within the household and he feels he has been *"deceived"* by the Moor.

Having witnessed the death of Roderigo, he later acts as a commentator, finding letters in Roderigo's pocket, revealing Iago's treachery.

As a man of honour and duty, he neatly concludes the play, demanding Othello be arrested, before the Moor takes his own life, and leaves Cyprus under the governorship of Cassio. His last lines, a rhyming couplet, reveal he is to return to Venice,

> *"And to the state*
> *This heavy act with heavy heart relate."*

Lodovico survives to tell the world of the tragedy and instructs Cassio to decide what punishment should befall Iago.

Section 1.10: The Duke of Venice

This minor character is the voice of reason. The duke has official authority in Venice and has two roles: to thwart invasion by the Turk and to arbitrate over Brabantio's claim that Othello has *"stol'n"* and bewitched his daughter.

The duke has great respect for Othello and on hearing of a threat of war declares,

> *"Valiant Othello, we must straight away employ you against the general enemy Ottoman".*

He is a fair man, giving Othello opportunity to speak in his defence against Brabantio's accusations of employing *"witchcraft"* to seduce Desdemona. He asks the Moor,

> *"What in your own part, can you say to this?"*

and Othello tells him how he did woo Desdemona, not with *"witchcraft"*, but with *"words"*.

The duke is so taken with Othello's story he comments,

> *"I think this tale would win my daughter too",*

and tells Brabantio he needs to accept what has happened. He holds Othello in great regard telling the outraged father,

> *"Your son-in-law is far more fair than black".*

The duke has more pressing business and instructs Othello to prepare for Cyprus and it is up to Othello whether Desdemona accompany him or not. He is wise enough to know not to interfere in matters between husband and wife.

Although a very minor role, the duke's favour on Othello contrasts sharply with Iago's opinion voiced to Brabantio via animal insults, comparing the Moor to a *"horse"*, a *"jennet"* and a *"ram"*. Lodovico is the voice of reason, of justice and authority. Should his word override that of an ancient?

Section 1.11: Montano

Montano was the former governor of Cyprus who, having served under Othello, praises him.

"The man commands like a full soldier",

he says, as he waits for the arrival of the Venetian ships. He greets Cassio and learns Othello is

"lost on a dangerous sea."

Tension builds, but Montano wishes to hear of Othello's new wife and Cassio obliges.

Later, Montano questions Iago about Cassio's drinking.

"Is he often thus?"

he enquires, when Cassio is drunk and Iago spins his *"web"* of lies. Montano is then injured in the brawl machinated between Roderigo and Cassio, proving Iago does not have full control over the consequences of his actions.

Montano appears again in Act V to condemn Iago as a *"monstrous"* villain, but he seems to have forgotten he was one who was

"led by the nose"

by Iago, having misjudged Cassio.

Section 1.12: Gratiano

This gentleman only appears in the final act to witness the chaos of Roderigo's assassination and Desdemona's demise. His presence, alongside that of Lodovico, is a reminder of the cultured Venetian way of life, in contrast to the heinous events in Cyprus.

Being a kinsman of Brabantio, he comes with news of the death of Desdemona's father, informing those present

*"Poor Desdemona, I'm glad your father's dead
Thy match was mortal to him, and pure grief shore his thread in twain."*

It transpires Brabantio died of a broken heart due to his daughter's inter-racial marriage.

Section Two: Themes

Section 2.1: The Theme of Jealousy

The exploration of the human emotion, jealousy, is the thrust of the play, *Othello*. Shakespeare demonstrates how jealousy is a solely destructive force, conveying the factors which provoke jealousy: anger, love and ambition.

Shakespeare's famous metaphor of jealousy being the *"green-ey'd monster"* certainly applies to Othello, who, despite his intentions, becomes a *"monster"*, literally and figuratively sick with jealousy and whose fortune turns because of it.

At the beginning of the play Othello is full of love and affection for Desdemona, has promoted Cassio, and speaks highly of *"honest Iago"*. His overall temperament is of goodwill and Desdemona is convinced Othello is incapable of jealousy.

> *"I think the sun where he was born drew all such humours from him"*,

she tells Emilia and, ironically, Othello's jealousy is partially brought about through love.

The Moor's character rapidly changes as Iago causes him to doubt Desdemona's fidelity and distrust Cassio, to a point of ostracising him. Iago puts

> *"jealous confirmations strong as proofs of Holy Writ"*

in Othello's path by leaving the handkerchief, the token Othello first gave Desdemona of his love, in *"Cassio's lodging"*. As Othello becomes a murderous monster, Shakespeare proves jealousy is an exclusively destructive force, destroying the life of the innocents: Cassio and Desdemona resulting in Othello's *"epilepsy"*, dreadful remorse and subsequent suicide.

> *"Farewell the tranquil mind"*

Othello laments, as Iago puts images into his head of Cassio's kisses on his wife's lips and, Othello's character completely turns. He becomes obsessively jealous of Desdemona's relationship with Cassio.

Roderigo is also jealous of the love Desdemona has for Othello and not for him. This jealousy is compounded when he hears of Desdemona's marriage to Othello. He is distraught and says,

> *"I will incontinently drown myself"*

and he seeks a petty revenge by telling Desdemona's father of the marriage. His love for Desdemona is then used by Iago to manipulate the gullible Venetian into picking a fight with Cassio, thus bringing about Cassio's fall from grace. Even when Roderigo doubts his desire to kill Cassio saying,

> *"I have no great devotion to the deed",*

he is spurred on by Iago's words that have ignited his jealousies.

Bianca is jealous when she finds the handkerchief in Cassio's quarters, arousing suspicions that he has received the token from *"a newer friend"*. The handkerchief has been the provocation for Othello's jealousy, when he suspects his wife of infidelity. (The handkerchief is decorated with *"strawberries"*, a fruit associated with romance; the colour red a symbol of sexuality.) Thereby love becomes a root cause of jealousy. Iago knows this and abuses the knowledge. There are other reasons, however to provoke jealousy.

It is Iago's jealousy of Cassio's promotion and Othello's command that incites Iago on his insidious quest to destroy both men.

> *"A fellow almost damn'd in a fair wife, that never set a squadron in the field"*

an enraged Iago spits, angry a supposed womaniser and soldier, who has seen little or no action on the battlefield, has been promoted above himself. Iago's subsequent manipulations are fuelled by his anger with Othello's choice of lieutenant. Thus, thwarted ambition is the root of Iago's jealousy and sets in motion his revenge.

It can be argued, however, that Iago is also jealous of Cassio and Othello due to love or lust, as he believes Othello and Cassio have bedded Emilia, his wife.

> *"He has done my office",*

Iago states of Othello and

> *"I fear Cassio with my night-cap too",*

but then goes on to say,

> *"I know not if't be true, but I, for mere suspicion of the kind, will do as if for surety."*

Thus revealing Iago's belief in Cassio's infidelity and his jealousy toward the Moor are equally ill-founded. The powerful emotion of jealousy overcomes all reason.

Jealousy is viewed as a madness and sickness by Iago, who realises Othello will become ill thinking Cassio has seduced Desdemona.

> *"I'll put the Moor into a jealousy so strong that judgement cannot cure",*

he schemes. The tragedy of the play hinges on this manipulation. Iago is well aware of the destruction jealousy can cause and how it can make man *"mad"* forcing him to act irrationally.

Ironically, when in a more rational state of mind both men equate jealousy with absurd behaviour.

"Good heaven, the souls of all my tribe defend from jealousy"

Iago cries and Othello agrees with him, declaring,

"Exchange me for a goat...away with love and jealousy".

Both men believe themselves to be men of reason, but Iago's hatred and Othello's jealousy are the undoing of them both.

Ambition and love are the causes for man to become jealous, angry, vengeful and hateful. Notice the irony here, how from goodness, evil can spring and how deep-rooted emotions can conquer reason.

The further irony is four hundred years after Shakespeare first performed the play, jealousy is still a destructive force, capable of overtaking man's rationality and reason. Is it not about time humankind learned?

Section 2.2: The Theme of Emotion versus Reason

Shakespeare was a fine observer of human nature and in several of his plays he proposes man is above the rest of the animal kingdom because of his ability to reason. Shakespeare noticed, however, that rational thought was often surpassed by intense passions or emotions and there are instances even today when a man's feelings cause him to act in an unprecedented manner

<u>Love overcoming reason</u>
'Love is blind' the old adage states. In some cases it can be considered to make some deaf and dumb as well! Such is the case for Othello and Desdemona. The couple truly love each other deeply, but Shakespeare insinuates if love is too intense, people distort the realities of life. Consider how Desdemona cannot see Othello's jealousy and Othello cannot see Desdemona's innocence. Iago says in soliloquy,

*"His soul is so enfetter'd to her love,
That she may make, unmake, do what she list",*

implying Othello's love for his wife makes him a puppet in her hands.

It is Iago who propounds Shakespeare's observation that an intense passion will eventually fade. Iago tells Roderigo,

"With what violence she first loved the Moor",

but

"her delicate tenderness will begin to heave the gorge".

Iago suggests Desdemona and Othello will soon become sick of feelings of intense passion. Shakespeare's warning (noted too in *Romeo and Juliet*) declares a passionate, lustful relationship will soon fade, possibly into that of Emilia's and Iago's relationship, where Emilia is treated as *"food"* for Iago's sexual appetites.

Desdemona reciprocates Othello's passion and this distracts her from rational thought, not seeing his true character. She recognises his intelligence and wisdom when he deals with the duke, the senators and affairs of state, but denies her husband is prone to jealousy. She is completely confused when she is faced with Othello in a mood.

> *"Why do you speak so startlingly and rash?"*

she questions and concludes,

> *"My lord is not my lord".*

Shakespeare shows that love can sometimes only see the good in a partner, not the bad.

In other scenes of the play it is shown how Desdemona is likely to succumb to her passions. Emilia recognises *"she'll run mad"* when Desdemona finds Othello's *"handkerchief"* has gone missing. Emilia knows her friend and mistress is quite love-struck and she is well acquainted with the effect love has on women. She tells of how

> *"a lady in Venice would have walked barefoot to Palestine for a touch of [Lodovico's] nether lip".*

Ironically even Desdemona tells of how her mother's maid *"prov'd mad"* when her lover *"did forsake her"*. Poor Desdemona cannot see how her love blinds her to life around her, her husband's jealousy and the sad fact love can drive men and women to distraction, causing a sickness or form of madness.

It is because Desdemona loves her husband so much that her death is credible. Even on her deathbed she shows her husband deference and tenderness. She is still almost blind to his intentions, not believing he will actually kill her. Desdemona's reason has thus been overtaken by love. She still wishes to see the good in her husband.

Roderigo, whose

> *"love has turned almost the wrong side out"*,

is also blinded by his feelings. Like others, Roderigo sees Desdemona through rose coloured glasses.

> *"She is full of most blessed condition"*

he sighs and has lost reasonable consideration of any faults she may have. Despite Desdemona's marriage to Othello, he still listens to Iago's words believing he has a chance to woo her if the marriage falls apart. Love has made Roderigo a *"fool",* manifested in his misjudgement of Iago.

Ironically, Iago tells Roderigo to use his *"wit"* in his dealings with him, and to realise he has Roderigo's best interests at heart. Roderigo is gullible, falling for Iago's flattery and lies. Only at the end of the play does the gentleman begin to reason and suspect Iago has abused him, robbing him of his money and setting him up as a murderer.

There is little passionate love between Emilia and Iago. Their marriage has become a relationship where *"love's first bloom"* has died. They are no longer blinded by love. Emilia is capable of seeing the reality of her husband's character. This highlights Shakespeare's theme to *"love moderately"* as he proclaims in *Romeo and Juliet*.

In complete contrast to the general theme that intense love overcomes reason and makes men blind or fools, Othello believes Desdemona has brought an order into his life.

> *"When I love thee not, chaos is come again"*,

he states. This proves to be a fitting prophecy, as indeed chaos reigns when his love is overcome by jealousy, not by reason.

Jealousy overcoming reason

Othello proves jealousy only breeds resentment, bitterness and hatred, resulting in tragic destruction.

Jealousy overcomes Othello's reason to the extent that he cannot see Desdemona's innocence, yet ironically, when rational, Othello can see the ruination of jealousy. He tells Iago,

> *"exchange me for a goat when I shall turn the business of my soul to such exsufflicate and blown surmises".*

But Othello allows his *"surmises"* of Desdemona's supposed infidelity to inflame his jealousy, which Iago relishes.

> *"The Moor already changes with my poison",*

he gloats and wishes Othello to suffer. He claims a

> *"little act upon the blood, burn like the mines of sulphur".*

The imagery of hell highlights Iago's hatred, seen also when Iago hopes

> *"Othello shall go mad".*

Othello's first onset of madness brought about by jealousy is seen when he raves,

> *"Farewell the tranquil mind, farewell content!"*

and again when his mind is torn.

> *"I think my wife be honest and think she is not",*

he tells Iago. The Moor is in such a state of jealous torment he becomes physically ill, falling *"into an epilepsy".*

Shakespeare was very interested in the means by which people lose their reason and become *"mad".* Although madness is not a prevalent theme in this play, Shakespeare explores how heightened emotions can lead to physical symptoms. (Consider how many feel physically sick and have a desire to go to the toilet when worried or anxious before exams.)

Prejudice overcoming reason
Another emotion that is often completely unreasonable is prejudice. Brabantio refuses to recognise Othello's nobility and position as a suitable husband for his daughter as his reason is blinded by his racial prejudice. "A Moor!" he bewails on hearing of Desdemona and Othello's marriage and he feels betrayed by his daughter.

"O treason of the blood"

he cries, wishing vengeance on Othello; his thoughts completely focused on his daughter's husband being black skinned, not on Othello's integrity.

Brabantio is so angered by what he views as a betrayal he brings Othello to the duke's court, where his emotions are assuaged, but he still feels deceived by Desdemona, despite her protestations that her love for the Moor is genuine. Consider how, even today, individuals are judged on their gender, race or religion. Sweeping assumptions of a person's character can be based on a generalisation not on rational thought. Iago states Moors have *"changeable wills"* in the same way female blondes are derided as brainless!

Shakespeare shows humanity has a tendency to judge on appearance and inevitably will be proven wrong. Despite Shakespeare's warnings in many of his plays, people persist in the almost innate reaction to judge others at first sight; thus be wary of the consequences of quick judgements.

Revenge overcoming reason
A major thrust of the action in *Othello* is the desire for revenge, which can overcome rational thought. Once Othello has *"proof"* of Cassio's desire for Desdemona, he calls for vengeance.

> *"Arise black vengeance from the hollow hell",*

he roars and his enraged jealousy spurs him to avenge those whom he believes have betrayed him, culminating in the desire to murder his wife.

> *"Let her rot and be damned tonight...*
> *I will chop her into messes",*

he raves, having lost all rational thought.

Despite Iago's ability to reason and calculate the downfall of Cassio, Othello and Roderigo, it can be argued his passions have led him to believe falsehoods. His jealousy at the thought of Othello and Cassio having bedded Emilia makes him vengeful and thus his soul will only be content when he has *"even'd"* with them. Emilia tells her husband

> *"some such squire he was that 'turn'd your wit the seamy side without, and made you suspect me with the Moor",*

implying Iago was overcome by emotional jealousy and lost his reason when he accused his wife of adultery.

The only other time Iago's emotions are tempered is in the final act when accused of his insidious deceit by his wife. He stabs Emilia in an act of desperation to silence her with the words, *"villainous whore"*. His vengeance against her betrayal is swift. He does not stop to reason a means to prevent her revelations.

Alcohol overcoming reason
Shakespeare was well acquainted with the fact alcohol could dull a man's reason. (His contemporary, Marlowe, was killed in a drunken brawl, and in many of his plays he refers to alcohol as being a means to dull the *"wits"*).

Cassio is fully aware of his inability to hold his liquor.

> *"I have very poor and unhappy brains for drinking",*

he tells Iago, who then uses the knowledge to his benefit, making Cassio drunk, resulting in a fight with Roderigo and his subsequent demotion.

Cassio laments,

> *"O God, that men should put an enemy in their mouths to steal away their brains",*

and wishes

> *"courtesy would invent some other custom of entertainment"*

rather than drinking. He berates himself for having succumbed to the effects of alcohol.

The irony is Othello has declared the men should celebrate the victory over the Turks and allowed the men to drink.

The Voices of Reason

In contrast to the emotive acts of the characters, there are moments of reason and clarity in the play.

Iago is reasoned and calculating in his actions in order to bring down Cassio, Roderigo and Othello. This is what makes him such a frightening, insidious villain. He is not crazed, but rational in his methods, acting on opportunity, planning his *"web"* and manipulating others.

In his first soliloquy Iago proves he is well aware of how man's emotions can overcome reason and cause them to do terrible deeds.

> *"If the balance of our lives had not one scale of reason to poise another sensuality, the blood and baseness of our natures would conduct us to most preposterous conclusions,"*

he states and reminds Othello sagely,

> *"As men in rage strike those that wish them best".*

He realises men in anger will *"strike"* even their closest family and friends.

Due to his observation of Othello, Iago knows

> *"the Moor is of a free and open nature ... and will as tenderly be led by the nose as asses are."*

Iago's ability to reason, to see traits in others and abuse them, makes him a calculating, dangerous, yet fascinating villain.

In the final scenes Iago sees, whatever way his plan works out, Roderigo and Cassio will both be killed, either by each other or by a little interference on his part. He stabs Roderigo, mortally wounding him, but his plan falls awry when Cassio is not killed. Despite his reasoning he cannot control all circumstances.

Iago's rationale does give him the value of foresight. He is fully aware the night of Desdemona's demise

> *"will either make me or fordoes me quite"*.

He is even rationally prepared for failure.

Iago's calculating mind is well documented when he manages to contradict himself arguing both sides of a debate. When Cassio laments the loss of his *"reputation"* Iago is quick to tell him,

> *"Reputation is an idle and most false imposition, oft got without merit"*,

but he argues the opposite with Othello.

> *"He that filches from me my good name.... makes me poor indeed"*,

he claims. Such is the workings of Iago's mind; he can think laterally and spin *"a web"* of deceit very easily.

At the beginning of the play the Duke of Venice is the voice of reason. He is arbiter between Othello and Brabantio when Brabantio accuses Othello of stealing his daughter. The Duke is also the main character in the instigation of war against the Turks. The senators and the duke see the threat of *"a Turkish fleet"* on its way to Cyprus and decide to stall its attack.

The duke is also aware Othello is a man capable of reason. He tells Brabantio,

> *"Your son-in-law is far more fair than black"*,

and this is seen when Othello holds judgement over Cassio's disgraceful drunken behaviour. Othello knows his *"blood"* and *"passion"* must not cloud his *"best judgement"* and listens to Iago's testimony as to what happened.

Othello's other voice of reason is that he wishes to see *"proof"* of Cassio's dalliance with Desdemona. Othello believes the old adage 'seeing is believing'.

> *"Make me see't; or at the least, so prove it, that the probation bear no hinge nor loop to hang a doubt on"*,

he tells Iago, but Othello's display of rationality only stresses the tragedy of his descent into *"a fit"*.

In his final words Othello seems to regain his reason. He asks those present to remember him well and not with

> *"malice...Must you speak of one that lov'd wisely but too well; of one not easily jealous, but, being wrought perplex'd in the extreme"*.

His words show a deep regret and he stabs himself, the noble gesture of a warrior.

Emilia at the end of the play is, like Othello, both emotive and reasoned. Her reason is shown in her discussion with

Desdemona about adultery. She views men and women as equally prone to their emotions and is enraged with her husband for being a deceitful liar. She is further angered by Othello's murder of Desdemona, but equally grief stricken. Yet, despite this turmoil of emotions, Emilia realises her husband's treachery.

"The Moor's abused by some most villainous knave",

she cries, deducing her husband's culpability.

Lodovico is a man of rational thought who contrasts with the emotive characters in the play. Shakespeare's audience would have equated a Venetian gentleman with civilised behaviour and cultured reason. When Lodovico notes Othello's action in striking his wife

"would not be believ'd in Venice"

and he is appalled by Othello's change in character.

"Is this the noble nature whom passion could not shake?"

he demands and regrets he has been *"deceived in him"*.

It is left for Lodovico to ask Cassio to devise the methods by which Iago should be punished and thus the play concludes.

Aristotle wrote three thousand years ago,

"The law is reason, free from passion".

The philosopher was well aware that, to decide the fate of others, man must be impartial. It is for the audience to decide on Iago's punishment. Will those watching the play do so rationally or will their emotions invade their judgement?

"Tho' this be madness yet there is method in it",

Polonius states in *Hamlet* and Shakespeare picks up on the rationality exhibited in Othello's madness, seen in the final act as he prepares to kill his wife. He reasons,

"she must die, else she'll betray more men",

suggesting he is preventing further suffering. He also wishes for her to die in a State of Grace, asking,

"Have you prayed tonight?"

and, in a moment of tenderness, says,

"I that am cruel am yet merciful; I would not have thee linger in thy pain",

thus showing some concern and lucidity. Even his own suicide seems to be the act of a rational man.

"For in my sense it is happiness to die",

he declares and asks Cassio and Lodovico to question Iago.

"Will you, demand that demi devil why he hath thus ensnar'd my soul and body?"

In his dying moments Othello's reason returns, but Shakespeare has proven that excessive emotions can easily lead to tragedy.

Conclusion

Shakespeare gives his audience much to ponder of human behaviour in *Othello*. What causes emotional outbursts? Do emotions or alcohol cloud judgement? What emotions overpower reason? Is mankind rational? Even four hundred years after the first dramatisation of the play, *Othello* is warning audiences to observe their own actions and those of others.

Section 2.3: Theme of Appearance versus Reality

The theme of appearance versus reality is one of the major concerns of the play *Othello*. How the characters appear often belies the reality of their true nature. Shakespeare very much plays on his audiences' stereotypical expectations.

Othello, for instance, is derided, via animal imagery, before an audience even see him. Iago calls him a *"black ram"* and a *"Barbary horse"*. When he initially appears on stage, he should be dressed in soldierly garb, but with regal bearing, after all, he is referred to as *"noble Othello"*. He is held in great regard by the duke when he states,

> *"Valiant Othello, we must straight employ you against the general enemy"*.

The duke realises the Moor's knowledge of Cyprus makes him the right man for command against the invading *"Turk"*.

Othello's eloquence of speech evokes an intelligence and gentility that would have surprised Shakespeare's audience. When he explains how he and Desdemona fell in love, his words are erudite and lyrical.

> *"It was my hint to speak ..*
> *Of the cannibals that each other eat,*
> *The Anthropophagi, and men whose heads*
> *Do grow beneath their shoulders."*

These are not the utterances of a *"savage"*, a barbarian, but of a well-travelled man, erudite man.

Sadly, under Iago's influence and manipulation, the Moor loses his reason, culminating in the murder of Desdemona. His final words recall his earlier eloquence when he asks to be remembered as

> *"one that loved not wisely but too well"*.

The Moor reminds audiences not to judge by a person's appearance and not to let their prejudices conquer their reason.

Initially viewers would be deceived by Iago's appearance. In the very first scene he may look like a Venetian soldier, but his words reveal a jealous heart. He mocks his general,

> *"'For Certes,' says he, "I have already chose my officer'"*,

then derides a fellow soldier, *"Michael Cassio"*, as an *"arithmetician"*.

The audience can be forgiven if confused, as Iago has a wonderful turn of phrase, but he blatantly tells Roderigo,

> *"I am not what I am"*,

thus warning the audience his appearance belies the reality of his true motivations and feelings.

Iago's success in his deception is due to his ability to hide his hate and desire for revenge behind a mask of honesty and sincerity. He speaks the truth when he ironically, warns Othello of

> *"the green-ey'd monster which doth mock the meat it feeds on"*,

but is cunning enough to know the passion of jealousy will undo Othello's reason.

Othello repeatedly calls his ancient *"honest Iago"*, highlighting Othello's flaw of trusting the man too much and not being able to see the reality behind Iago's appearance. He should appear in a production well dressed, well spoken and of good comportment. Desdemona and Cassio too are fooled into believing Iago *"an honest fellow"*.

The fascination of Iago's appearance, which belies the reality, is seen in his soliloquies. In these the audience becomes fully aware of Iago's true nature and villainy, betraying and deceiving others. This adds greatly to the tension and the tragedy of the play.

In soliloquy he speaks openly and honestly.

> *"I hate the Moor"*,

he spits and admits he will play Roderigo for

> *"sport and profit"*,

which he does, taking the gullible man's *"fortune"*.

Roderigo thus becomes a part of the appearance versus reality theme. He should appear as a Venetian gentleman. Shakespeare's audience would then expect the man to be cultured and educated. Love has made *"a fool"* of Roderigo and the audience learns his appearance belies his foolishness when he parts with his money. Furthermore, he is skilfully manipulated to do Iago's bidding and becomes enmeshed in a brawl, hardly the actions expected of a gentleman.

Brabantio's prejudice against a man who he *"invited"* into his home is not expected of a gentleman either. Desdemona's father has been host to Othello for considerable time, urging him to tell

> *"the story of [his] life...even from [his] boyish days"*.

It is not the act of a gentleman to be host to a man and then deride him for marrying his daughter. Brabantio dies of a broken heart because he is unable reconcile his bias with the love his daughter bears for a *"black"* man.

Desdemona's appearance is described by several of the male characters. Cassio esteems her as *"a maid that paragons description and wild fame".*

Roderigo worships her as a woman of

"beauty, wit and fortunes"

and Othello believes she is *"my soul's joy"* and will *"deny [her] nothing"*.

But Desdemona exhibits a forceful independent streak, initially shown when she decides to marry the Moor without her father's consent. Even Iago states she is the *"general"* of Othello and she is quite resilient when she asks the duke permission to accompany her husband to Cyprus.

"Let me go with him,"

she states and is supported by Othello.

When dealing with her husband she speaks her mind demanding when they can discuss Cassio's demotion.

"Why then tomorrow night, or Tuesday morn;
On Tuesday noon, or night, on Wednesday morn.
I prithee name the time, but let it not
Exceed three days."

A segment of Desdmona's tragedy is the conflict she suffers between being an independent spirit and an obedient wife.

Emilia also defies the expectations of Shakespeare's audience. Wives were expected to be dutiful, loving, loyal and demure, deferring to their husbands. Emilia exhibits a worldly intelligence with regard to men, accusing them of using women as *"food"* to sate their lecherous *"appetites"* and blaming them for leading women astray.

"The ills we do, their ills instruct us so",

she claims, propounding if men ill-treat their women, then like men, they will want their *"revenge".*

In contrast, other characters in the play are exactly what they appear to be. Bianca is the put upon prostitute, the duke and Lodovico the voices of reason, stereotypical of politicians. It is because these minor characters conform to stereotypes, the audience is duped by the appearance of others.

Section 2.4: The Theme of Deception, Deceit and Betrayal

Iago's character is often viewed as Shakespeare's most odious villain because of his deceitful, insidious personality and his lack of remorse. The theme of deception very much surrounds him and his relationship with the other characters. Othello, Brabantio, Cassio, Desdemona, Roderigo and even Emilia, are all deceived by Iago.

Like Othello and Roderigo, Cassio trusts Iago, acting on his instructions to ask Desdemona to speak on his behalf to Othello following his demotion. Iago tells Cassio,

"Our general's wife is now our general... she'll help put you in your place again."

Later, Cassio is betrayed and Iago relishes the moments when he sees Cassio pay homage to Desdemona, knowing that, as Cassio touches the lady's hand, the destruction of Cassio (and Othello) is imminent.

"With as little a web as this will I ensnare as great a fly as Cassio",

Iago gloats, as his plan unfolds. The spider / fly / web imagery vividly conveys the patient, malignant Iago's desire to destroy his victims.

Iago's success in betraying his fellow men is also due to his ability to recognise flaws in others and then use the knowledge for his own gain. Iago fully uses Othello's flaw to turn him literally mad. He recognises Roderigo's gullibility and Cassio's self-pity when he loses his *"reputation"*. Via this knowledge he spins his *"web"* of deceit and treachery.

This *"web"* even extends to betraying his wife by using her to steal the *"handkerchief"*, Othello's first gift to Desdemona. Although it is ambiguous as to how deeply Emilia is misled by her husband, when she says

> "what he will do with it heaven knows, not I".

Emilia later betrays her husband by revealing the theft and Iago's deceitful *"villainy"* in her dying breath. There is a cosmic symmetry in one spouse betraying the other.

It can be argued Iago is lucky in the manner in which his plans come to pass, but consider how Iago is an opportunist, acting to his own advantage on every available occasion. In the opening scene Brabantio is enraged by Iago's words,

> "An old black ram is tupping your white ewe"

metaphorically describing Othello and Desdemona's lovemaking. Iago has a wonderful turn of phrase, knowing exactly what to say in order to incense others. He intends to enrage Brabantio to act against Othello and destroy him. Iago does not need to dirty his own hands when there are others to do his bidding!

Iago's deceit and deception are a result of his quick wittedness and resourcefulness. He manipulates Cassio into drinking far more than he initially wished and thus provokes a fight between Cassio and Roderigo, resulting in Cassio's demotion. He is quick to act underhandedly in a fight, shouting out *"Murder"* to distract others while he himself is committing the crime of slaying Roderigo.

He is sympathetic when Desdemona weeps because Othello believes she has *"offended"* her husband. He is laughably insincere in his question,

> "How comes this trick upon him?"

and then lies, saying it is the *"business of state"* which has upset him.

Roderigo pays Iago to become a suitor to Desdemona,

despite her marriage. Iago leads Roderigo astray, knowing his emotions will overcome his reason, ultimately killing him and betraying him. Although Roderigo has his doubts about Iago at times, he is so blinded by his desire for Desdemona he overlooks Iago's malignant nature.

Iago's treachery creates tension and suspense within the play.

"I hate the Moor ....
He hold me well; the better shall my purpose work on him",

he states and the audience becomes aware of Iago's intent to deceive and to betray the unsuspecting Othello. As he abuses Othello's trust so the audience become sympathetic toward the Moor. Consider when Iago manipulates a situation whereby Othello overhears a conversation between Cassio and Iago. As Cassio speaks of Bianca, Othello believes he is speaking of Desdemona. Furthermore, Iago makes remarks about Cassio's gestures to Desdemona in Othello's presence.

"Mark the fleers, the gibes and notable scorns that dwell in every region of his face",

he tells poor, jealous Othello.

Iago is the personification of deceit, dishonesty and insidiousness and Shakespeare employs contrast to highlight Iago's wickedness. Othello finds it extremely difficult to lie and deceive.

"O hardness to dissemble",

he cries aside, when he tells his wife he is

"Well, my good lady",

but is really upset with the thoughts of her alleged adultery. Othello's integrity only makes the tragedy of Desdemona's assassination, and his fall and ultimate demise even more poignant.

Although Iago is the central character with regard to deception there are other instances of betrayal to consider.

Brabantio feels betrayed by his daughter when she chooses to marry Othello behind his back. Brabantio in turn hopes to betray Othello by bringing him before the duke, but this is thwarted when the duke decides in Othello's favour. Yet he warns Othello,

> "She has deceiv'd her father; and may thee".

Has Desdemona deceived her father, or is Brabantio angry because she has married a man he considers unworthy without his consent?

Betrayal in marriage is also considered. Iago hates Othello not only because he has promoted Cassio before him, but because he suspects Othello has bedded his wife. The sin of adultery is brought to the fore in this play, a betrayal of the marriage vow where a spouse swears to 'forsake all others'. In Shakespeare's time it was accepted by the nobility that men would have mistresses and prostitution was a trade plied openly in the streets. Shakespeare forces his audience to consider the hypocrisy of men who vow to remain faithful, but openly kept other women for *"sport"*.

The theme of deception very much revolves around Iago and the consequence of his actions lead to the tragic deaths of Desdemona, Othello, Roderigo and Emilia. Cassio is left to decide the punishment for this cold-hearted, calculating villain, who confesses his treachery, but then refuses to ever *"speak word"* ensuring the theme of justice and retribution is closely linked with betrayal. How low a villain is Iago? Is his insidious, deceitful nature the worst of human failings? How can a person realise they are being deceived? These are the questions Shakespeare raises as his audience watches and re-views his play.

Section 2.5: The Theme of Love and Duty

The theme of love and duty in *Othello* is closely related to the theme of jealousy, love being a root cause of jealousy. Shakespeare also urges his audience to think of how the powerful emotion of love can overcome reason; the choices love forces characters to make; how love cannot be bought, and the concept of filial duty versus spousal duty arises when Desdemona has to choose between the love she bears her father and her love for Othello.

The Ancient Greeks had a number of words for love. In today's society the word is used to mean a number of things, none of which evoke the same feeling at all. 'I love chocolate cake' does not convey the same emotion as 'I love my mother', which in turn does not convey the same intensity of passion as 'I love my boyfriend / girlfriend nor the same commitment as 'I love my husband / wife'. Love has become an overused word in the English language and the study of Shakespeare allows the audience to consider the value of love, the meaning of love and the consequences of love.

Consider Othello and Desdemona's marriage, which is based on romantic love. They have an idealistic union, which came about when Othello visited the house of Brabantio. There he

"spake of most disastrous chances, of moving accidents by flood and field"

which both entranced Brabantio and his daughter. Desdemona loves Othello because of

"the dangers [he] had pass'd",

thus she sees him as a romantic hero, a conqueror, a man of action and this vision of the man is somewhat clouded by youthful innocence. She loves him deeply and he loves her, but neither have a realistic view of marriage, which, ironically, is obscured by their passion. Tragically their love overcomes their reason.

Brabantio considers Othello and Desdemona's marriage as

> *"too true an evil .... against all rules of nature"*

wherein his daughter has been

> *"abus'd stol'n and corrupted".*

Brabantio believes Othello has bewitched his daughter with *"witchcraft"* and Desdemona has betrayed him.

> *"She has deceived her father and may thee",*

he warns Othello and Iago later reminds Othello of Desdemona's betrayal.

The concept of betraying a parent is in league with filial duty, which arises in Act I. In several of Shakespeare's plays the conflict between a child's duty to a parent, propounded in the fifth Commandment, versus the marriage vow, is raised. Desdemona states she

> *"perceive[s] here a divided duty:*
> *to you [Brabantio] I am bound for life and education",*

but she is also beholden to her husband. The marriage ceremony for a woman included the vow of obedience, thus for women the conflict arose as to whom they should show the greater obedience: parent or husband? Desdemona shows a greater allegiance to her husband, which enrages Brabantio, who emotes great prejudice in that his daughter has married a *"Moor"*.

Does Othello and Desdemona's marriage seem too good to be true, almost a fairy tale? Does their love blind them to the realities of marriage and each other? Desdemona is upset when Othello accuses her of being a *"whore"* and when he faces her demanding she show him the *"handkerchief"* he gave her. She sees a temper she did not expect claiming,

> *"My lord is not my lord."*

She then looks to Emilia and Iago to help her

> *"win my lord again"*.

It's as if this is her first experience of Othello's temper and she is at a loss as to what to do.

Compare the newly weds marriage to Iago and Emilia's. Their relationship is of much longer standing and is almost estranged. Iago degrades Emilia and women in general and she has a cynical view of men saying,

> *"they are all but stomachs and we all but food; they eat us hungrily"*.

Yet she remains faithful to her marriage vow when she tries to please Iago. When she finds the *"handkerchief"*, she dutifully gives it to her husband as he has so often begged for her to steal it. This allows Iago to ensure Othello's jealousy, although remember it is Othello's great love for Desdemona that also fuels the *"green-ey'd monster"*.

In the final act it is clear Emilia has a greater understanding of her husband than any other character. It is she who realises how he has deceived and manipulated Othello, accused Desdemona of adultery by telling

> *"an odious damn lie"*

and of Iago's *"villainy"*. She makes the courageous decision to break her vow of obedience when she ignores his pleas of *"hold your peace"* crying,

> *"No, I will speak as liberal as the north"*.

Iago's true feelings for his wife are then revealed when he mortally stabs her. Whatever love he had for her is overcome by self-preservation. Emilia dies an honourable death with the truth of Desdemona's innocence as her dying testimony. Is Iago and Emilia's relationship a more honest portrayal of love and marriage than Othello and Desdemona's?

Love as lust is documented in Bianca and Cassio's relationship. Cassio confesses he has not seen Bianca for

> *"eight score eight hours"*

(score = 20 therefore 8 x 20 + 8 = 168 = one week) and looks forward to their union, when Bianca should

> *"bring [him] on the way a little",*

suggesting a sexual dalliance is all Cassio has in mind. This is compounded later when he speaks to Iago about his relationship with Bianca being irksome.

> *"She falls about my neck ... hangs and lolls and weeps upon me",*

he complains and laughs at the suggestion of him marrying her. In fact he has more of a mind to *"leave her company"*. Shakespeare encourages the audience to consider men's use (or abuse) of women, playing with them for their *"sport"*.

Bianca does not view Cassio in the same lustful way, but is infatuated with him and is most distressed when Iago stabs him. (Iago makes the most of Bianca's presence by averting suspicions onto her.) Bianca and Cassio's relationship reveals a distinct difference between how men and women view love.

Roderigo's love for Desdemona is also a form of lust, but tinted with the delusion of a union between him and Desdemona can come to pass. Roderigo has pursued

Desdemona, but has been thwarted by Brabantio, therefore he has employed Iago, giving him money and jewels to ensure Desdemona will consider him as a suitor.

> *"Put money in thy purse,"*

Iago encourages Roderigo. Thus Shakespeare questions whether money can procure love. Iago allows Roderigo to believe he has a chance with Desdemona even when she is married, as he is sure

> *"Moors are changeable in their wills"*

and Desdemona

> *"When she is sated with his body she will find the errors of her choice"*,

suggesting the marriage will not last.

Like Othello, Roderigo sees Desdemona through rose coloured glasses.

> *"She is full of most blessed condition"*,

he sighs and, because of his desire to marry her, Roderigo allows himself to be used as a tool to kill Cassio. Once again Roderigo's love shows how men can allow their emotions to overcome their reason. Does love blind Roderigo to the fact the object of his affection is in love with another man?

Friendship is a form of love between two people and is explored in Desdemona's relationship with Cassio. She shows loving concern when Othello demotes him and Cassio displays an affection and respect for Desdemona, which Othello misinterprets as a display of romantic love. Cassio takes advantage of the friendship hoping Desdemona will speak with Othello on his behalf, putting him back in Othello's favour. Desdemona readily agrees.

> *"I will do all my abilities in thy behalf"*,

she tells him, but this is her undoing. Othello, thanks to Iago's *"poison"* and manipulation, doubts Desdemona's loyalty. Desdemona's friendship with Cassio thus is a factor in her demise. Shakespeare raises the question of how acts of friendship can be misconstrued and whether it is possible for a platonic relationship to exist between a man and a woman.

Although Emilia is Desdemona's inferior in the social hierarchy, there is a friendship between the two women. Emilia is older and more worldly wise, but has an affectionate regard for Desdemona's heartfelt love for Othello. She is aware, for example, that there are women who betray their husbands and commit adultery, but condemns the act stating she would not do it herself and

"risk purgatory for 't".

(Don't forget it is a sin, the breaking of the Seventh Commandment.)

Emilia sees husbands at fault

"if wives do fall",

suggesting husbands are responsible for the behaviour of their wives. This is an interesting idea to consider. Women in the 17th century had very few rights and were dependent on their husbands, thus were their actions a result of their husband's dereliction of duty? The concept that husbands are now responsible for the actions of their wives is almost alien in western society, where women are more independent. Do husbands still have a duty to their wives? Is that duty reciprocal?

Emilia is caught between a duty to her husband and a duty to her friend with regard to the finding of Desdemona's *"handkerchief"*. She is misguided when she gives it to Iago, but she regains her honour in death by dutifully standing by her friend and mistress, denouncing her treacherous husband.

In *Othello* the theme of love, duty and friendship are brought to the fore. Shakespeare encourages his audience to consider the means by which love can change a person; how it can bring great joy and great pain and how it can overcome reason. The relationships between men and women are explored; the concept of equality is touched upon and the differences and similarities between men and women are considered. Filial duty and duty to a spouse is worthy of study. Do the same principles apply today as in the 17th century? Friendship being misconstrued, friendship being put before marriage and whether love can be bought are also issues within the play. The joy of studying Shakespeare is in contemplating this universal theme and realising that, despite time differences, geographic locations and racial differences, love is a force to be reckoned with.

Section 2.6: The Theme of Prejudice

As the title character of *Othello* is a Moor, a man of coloured race, there is the expectation racism will be a theme of the play. However Shakespeare encourages his audience to consider other forms of prejudice: sexism and social hierarchy.

Racism
In the opening scene Iago refers to Othello as a *"black ram"* knowing this will enrage Brabantio's racial prejudices. The fact the father's *"white ewe"* is *"tupping"* the *"black ram"* is a vivid animal image of mixed race marriage. The insinuation is Desdemona has married beneath her.

Being a Moor, Othello is an alien within Venetian society, although ironically it is he who shows the courtesy and intellect expected from this prosperous and culturally advanced city. He is well spoken, well educated, well positioned in the military and is often called *"noble Othello"*, therefore is a fitting match for Desdemona in every other way.

The fact Othello has married a white woman is referred to as *"lascivious"* and Iago exploits the mixed marriage, by suggesting Desdemona has been unfaithful due to Othello's race and colour. He suggests there may be something *"unnatural"* or *"foul"* about Desdemona's attraction to a man who is not of similar *"complexion"* to herself.

> *"Not to affect may proposed matches*
> *Of her own clime, complexion, and degree,*
> *Whereto we see in all things, Nature tends:*
> *Foh, one may smell in such, a will most rank,*
> *Foul disproportions, thoughts unnatural."*

Shakespeare causes his audience to ponder why such a marriage is repugnant and why people judge others simply on the colour of a person's skin. Shakespeare considers too how people are judgemental of those who have shown great assistance in bettering or securing the larger world, but are loath to invite such into the enclave of a family.

Sexism

It is via Emilia that Shakespeare allows the audience to consider the similarities of men and women. One cannot help but draw parallels to Shylock's speech in *The Merchant of Venice* in which he puts forth similarities between Jews and Christians. Emilia states,

"Let husbands know their wives have sense like them; they see and smell"

then uses rhetorical questions to provoke similarities between men and women's sexual appetites.

"When they change us for others? Is it sport? …. Have we not affections? Desires for sport and frailty like men have?"

She then concludes,

"Let them use us well; else let them know, the ills we do, their ills instruct us so",

blaming men for teaching women bad behaviour.

Women were not equal to men in Renaissance England. They were viewed as inferior, the fairer and weaker sex. Shakespeare, via Emilia, puts forward an interesting argument that husbands are at fault *"if wives do fall"*. The argument is logical: if women are so weak and inferior surely husbands are responsible for the behaviour of their wives.

Emilia proves to be a very strong character, with an integrity that is belied when she first appears. Shakespeare showed that, like his former patron, Queen Elizabeth I, women were not inferior, brainless or weak. Elizabeth herself had to overcome a great deal of prejudice on her ascension to the throne, especially with regard to taking a husband. Instead she wedded herself to the Crown and reigned debatably better than any man. England certainly thrived under her rule.

Social Hierarchy
In Shakespeare's day it was widely believed that God dictated man's place on Earth. Any desire of aggrandisement via ambition was seen as a sin against God. There was a definite social hierarchy where the nobility reigned, and others were there to serve. During the Renaissance the feudal system of lords and serfs underwent a change due to an increase in trade and exploration. A middle class began to emerge by way of bankers and traders. Craftsmen gained a higher status than workers, but separate from this social hierarchy was the Church and the military. These had their own hierarchy and the military hierarchy is apparent in *Othello*.

Othello has gained his position in the military ranks due to his prowess on the battlefield. His subsequent defeat of the Turks in Cyprus is evidence of this. His honour and merit has been deserved and suitably rewarded. He also shows integrity and speaks of being

"from men of royal siege"

suggesting in his homeland he is of the nobility. The Duke of Venice greets him with the words, *"Valiant Othello"* and his counsel is sought often by the senate, placing him within the higher echelons of society.

Iago is embittered because Cassio has been promoted above him, believing Cassio to be less deserving. According to Iago, Cassio is

"A man ... that never set a squadron in the field, nor the division of a battle knows more than a spinster",

but he has been made Othello's lieutenant. Iago's discontent seems to be well placed when he explains he has served Othello

> *"at Rhodes, at Cyprus"*

and Cassio has merely been promoted because

> *"preferment goes by letter and affection, not by the old gradation,*
> *where each second stood heir to the first."*

Iago claims Othello has chosen Cassio due to favouritism, not because he was his second in command. Whether Iago is to be believed is a matter for debate.

In *Othello,* Shakespeare asks the nobility in his audience to consider their reasons for promoting men. It is a concept worthy of consideration in today's society where nepotism is still evident.

In the household of Othello, Emilia is Desdemona's inferior in the social hierarchy due to her husband's status. Emilia is older and more worldly wise, but has an affectionate regard for Desdemona's heartfelt love for Othello. Emilia is caught between a duty to her husband and a duty to her friend with regard to the finding of Desdemona's handkerchief. In the final act Emilia realises how her husband has deceived and manipulated Othello, accused Desdemona of adultery by telling

> *"an odious damn lie"*

and of his overall *"villainy"*. She then makes the courageous decision to break her marriage vow of obedience when she ignores his pleas of *"hold your peace"* and cries,

> *"No, I will speak as liberal as the north".*

With her dying breath, she declares Desdemona's innocence and her husband's treachery. Via Emilia Shakespeare makes his audience evaluate the strength of women and their divisive position in society.

Conclusion

The joy of studying Shakespeare is in contemplating universal themes and realising, despite time differences and geographic locations, very little has changed in the human situation. Prejudice was a part of the human situation in the 17th century, as it still is today four hundred years later.

Section 2.7: The Theme of Punishment, Justice and Retribution

The theme of punishment, justice and retribution is linked to the character of Iago and his involvement with other characters. Shakespeare opens up a number of questions for his audience to consider with regard to meting out punishment. Do not forget Shakespeare's noble audience would have been in positions of power, therefore would be concerned with justice on a daily basis.

Shakespeare included the theme of retribution and revenge in many of his plays to remind audiences revenge was cyclic and futile, (eg: *Romeo and Juliet*). During the Renaissance, in certain areas of Europe, acts of revenge were rife and it is a prominent theme in the Old Testament. Do not forget the Church was undergoing major changes at this time and although murder was not condoned, there were duels, feuds and civil conflicts that often never reached the courts. When studying this theme I consider the questions Shakespeare raises.

<u>Does Cassio deserve to be avenged / punished by Iago for being promoted?</u>
Iago is jealous as Cassio has been promoted above himself and because he believes that he has slept with his wife, Emilia.

> "For I fear Cassio with my nightcap too".

he says and believes Cassio's promotion is due to favouritism on the part of Othello.

Iago's act of revenge is self-serving. If he rids the army of Cassio, then he is most likely to take his place. Iago's ambition overtakes his reason in his quest for aggrandisement. He decides to put Cassio

> "in some action that may offend the isle",

therefore makes Cassio drunk, knowing that the man has

> "unhappy brains for drinking".

Iago masterfully manipulates Cassio into a brawl with Roderigo and this behaviour is subsequently punished by Othello.

The wisdom of showing favour to a close friend is questioned in this play. Iago laments that Cassio's experience is

> "mere prattle without practise is all his soldiership"

but is this reason enough for Iago to seek revenge?

The fact that Cassio lives and becomes governor is Shakespeare's way of showing good should conquer evil. As Cassio is the only character left alive at the end of the play who has been abused by Iago, is it only fitting he be the judge of Iago's punishment?

<u>Does Othello deserve to be avenged / punished for overlooking Iago's case for promotion?</u>
Iago admits,

> "I hate the Moor."

He is jealous of Othello's success and angry he has been overlooked for promotion. Iago also suspects the *"lusty Othello"* to have slept with his wife, and wishes to avenge him *"wife for wife"*. Thereby Iago seeks to destroy Othello.

In turn, Othello is completely oblivious to Iago's evil thoughts, mistakenly viewing his *"ancient"* as *"honest"*. Othello trusts him to the extent that he asks Iago to care for his wife while he is fighting the Turk.

> "My Desdemona I leave to thee",

he says.

Iago's twisted reasoning sees Othello as the enemy within and he believes the Moor should be punished for his oversight in promoting Cassio and not himself. His first spiteful act is to tell Brabantio of his daughter's marriage to the Moor in the hope Othello will be chastised. He hopes to *"poison"* Othello's *"delight"* in his marriage.

Shakespeare is reminding audiences that one must be careful in choices for promotion, to do it fairly and justly, not because of any form of favouritism. Nepotism was evident on a daily basis in Shakespeare's time and is still present society today.

<u>Does Desdemona deserve to be killed for her suspected adultery?</u>
Desdemona is viewed by most as the innocent victim of the play and the tragedy lies in that she is convicted of a sin she does not commit. Shakespeare wishes his audience to consider the concept of suspicion and proof.

Othello believes he has *"proof"* of Desdemona's betrayal when he sees Cassio with the *"handkerchief"* and overhears the contrived conversation between Iago and Cassio, believing they are speaking of Desdemona when they are actually speaking of Bianca. Iago being a master manipulator ensures Othello to believe Cassio to

"lie with her, lie on her"

and the betrayal sends Othello *"into an epilepsy"*.

Othello does ask Iago if Cassio *"confess it?"* but Iago's *"medicine"* to *"poison"* Othello's mind ensures Othello does not accuse Cassio face to face. Shakespeare wishes his audience to be careful in their decisions as to what is real and what is not and to be aware within criminal activity, lies and deceit abound.

<u>Does Roderigo deserve to die?</u>
Roderigo is a gullible fool, completely misled by Iago who

encourages him to

> *"put money in thy purse"*

and pursue Desdemona via precious gifts. Roderigo's reason is overcome by his desire for Desdemona, seeing her through rose tinted glasses.

> *"She is full of most blessed condition",*

he laments.

Roderigo's death is necessary to Iago for two reasons. Firstly, he does not wish to be caught for purloining the *"jewels"* meant for Desdemona and, secondly, he envisages Cassio being punished for Roderigo's murder. Roderigo may pay a heavy price for his gullibility and lust but Shakespeare urges his audience to consider how gullibility, foolishness and desire can lead to ruin.

Does Othello deserve his death?
Othello realises he has been betrayed by Iago and feels intensely guilty having killed an innocent woman. The tragedy of the play is that in complete remorse Othello takes his own life.

> *"Blow me about in winds! Roast me in sulphur! Wash me in steep-down gulfs of liquid fire!"*

he calls and although suicide can be considered a coward's way out, not living to face the consequences of one's actions, in Shakespeare's day it was viewed as the greatest sin against God, thus the soul would descend to hell. Othello's words create an image of the hell he faces.

The purpose of tragedy is for the hero to fall because of a flaw in his character (hamartia). Othello's intense jealousy brings about his ruin, but he has been abused, betrayed and manipulated by Iago. His foolishness in not being able to see Iago's true self is not reason enough for his demise. His crime is uxoricide and for that he should be punished. By committing suicide, Othello decides his own punishment.

Does Emilia deserve her death?
Like Othello, Iago commits the crime of uxoricide, but under completely different circumstances. Iago, in a desperate act to prevent Emilia from revealing the truth, stabs his wife, but Emilia's dying words reveals Iago's *"villainy"*.

> *"The handkerchief I found by fortune and did give my husband."*

Shakespeare's major question to consider is: How guilty is Emilia? Emilia chooses to give Iago Desdemona's love token with the words,

> *"what he will do with it heaven knows, not I"*

suggesting she is not aware of Iago's insidious plans. If that is the case then, like Desdemona, she becomes an innocent victim. If she is aware of Iago's intent then is death too strong a punishment for being an accessory?

What should Iago's punishment be?
Iago's guilt is beyond doubt. It is generally accepted Iago is the worst of Shakespeare's villains, not only for the havoc he creates, but because he shows absolutely no remorse for his actions. Dying in a graceless state will ensure his descent into hell, but Lodovico gives Cassio the right to decide Iago's earthly fate.

> *"To you lord governor, remains the censure of this hellish villain, the time, the place, the torture."*

The penalty for general murder during Shakespearean times was hanging, but there were other forms of punishment for different kinds of murder. Treason was punished by beheading (by axe of by sword), heresy meant burning at the stake, but there were also drownings for witchcraft, crushings and stonings; not to mention the many forms of torture invented by powerful individuals and the use of unprecedented machinery.

Shakespeare leaves Iago's earthly fate to the imagination of the audience, yet the audience would also have to remember not to let their emotions cloud their decision.

Humankind is still inventive in ways and means by which people are punished and tortured, and although in western civilisation people may see themselves as less barbaric than in days gone by, the question of crime and punishment, justice and retribution still remains.

Section Three: Imagery

Imagery is abundant in *Othello* to highlight themes, describe time and place and reveal character traits. There are several recurring images in the play: images of light and dark, sight and blindness, the image of disease and corruption, images of clothing, food, heaven and hell, as well as natural imagery and the image of magic, particularly within the handkerchief.

The use of imagery also appeals to an audience once the plot is understood. Spotting the subtle employment of images is good fun and heightens the text.

Imagery is most apparent in Iago's soliloquies thus, to learn more about the power of imagery, study these too.

Section 3.1: Images of Light and Dark

The theme of light and dark relates to the overall theme of good and evil.

The play begins at night when Roderigo and Iago wake Brabantio to tell him of his daughter's marriage to the Moor. The darkness of the scene highlights the malignancy of the act, as Brabantio becomes enraged with the news his daughter has lowered herself by marrying a black man. Brabantio's prejudice can thus be viewed as evil.

Darkness however tends to surround Iago, arguably the most evil villain of Shakespeare's plays. His hatred of the Moor is first muttered at night and in many productions his soliloquies are performed in shadow. The fight he first orchestrates between Roderigo and a drunken Cassio is at night, highlighting his deceitful nature.

In contrast good characters tend to be surrounded by light. When Cassio first appears he is bearing a torch, searching for Othello who is required by the senate because the Turk is waging an attack. The plans the senate makes are done under torchlight.

Light is also used in the sense to bring something out into the open. In soliloquy Iago plots to make Othello jealous and

"be led by the nose as asses are".

Iago swears to enact his revenge by stating that he will bring Othello's ruination to *"the world's light"*.

Emilia and Desdemona when chatting swear that they would bring adultery into *"Heavenly light"*, but Emilia quips she would not do it either in the dark. The concept is that adultery is evil, a sin.

In the final act the image of light and dark is most prevalent.

Roderigo is attacked by Iago at night, and hypocritically Iago later condemns men for killing others in *"the dark"*, a sign of a coward, an act of evil and he calls for *"light"* to be brought upon the scene. He later condemns Roderigo for setting upon Cassio *"in the dark"*.

Prior to killing his wife Othello literally brings *"light"* into the bedchamber by bearing a torch and demands the truth. He is prepared to

"put out the light",

a metaphor for killing Desdemona. However her *"light"* may be restored if she repents her sins and dies in a State of Grace thereby going to heaven. The image is of the light of God.

The arrival of Montano carrying a light into the bedchamber brings forth the other image of light, which is enlightenment. The final scene reveals the truth of Iago's machinations, Othello's mistakes, Emilia's involvement and the subsequent revelation of the truth of Desdemona's innocence.

The concepts of light and dark stress the good and evil within the play: the evil of prejudice, the evil of cowardice and Iago's villainy is emphasised by darkness.

The light of life is referred to by Othello, and the light of God is touched upon in that heaven will bring great solace to those who die in a State of Grace. The light of enlightenment is greatest in the final scene where the truth is revealed and Shakespeare also uses this image in the hope his audience have become enlightened as to the evils of mankind.

Section 3.2: Images of Sight and Blindness

The image of sight and blindness stresses the themes of appearance versus reality, prejudice, emotion versus reason and love.

When Desdemona asks to be allowed to accompany Othello to Cyprus, she says,

> *" I saw Othello's visage in his mind, and to his honours and his valiant parts did I my soul and fortunes consecrate".*

Othello's blackness, his visible difference from everyone around him, is of little importance to Desdemona. She has the power to see him for what he is in a way even Othello himself cannot. Unlike her father, she can see beneath her husband's *"sooty bosom"*.

Earlier in Act I, Scene III, a senator suggests the Turkish retreat to Rhodes is

> *"a pageant to keep us in false gaze"*.

Perhaps the Turks retreat is a trick, an appearance that belies a worrying reality.

The beginning of Act II consists entirely of people staring out to sea, waiting to see the arrival of ships, friendly or otherwise. War and subsequent celebration prevent the characters from seeing Iago's manipulations and the truth being enacted in front of them. Cassio is easily duped into drunkenness, Roderigo is gullible to Iago's flattery and Othello is easily made jealous.

Othello, although he demands *"ocular proof"*, is frequently convinced by things he does not see. He strips Cassio of his position as lieutenant based on the story Iago tells, he relies on Iago's tale of seeing Cassio wipe his beard with Desdemona's handkerchief and he believes Cassio to be dead simply because he hears him scream.

Roderigo is equally duped by Iago's flattery and lies; thus Shakespeare is warning his audience that seeing is believing and be careful whom to trust.

The action of the play depends heavily on characters not seeing things. Othello accuses his wife, although he never sees her infidelity, and Emilia, although she watches Othello erupt into a rage about the missing handkerchief, does not figuratively see what her husband has done until the final act when she rationalises Iago's villainy.

After Othello has killed himself in the final scene, Lodovico says to Iago,

> *"Look on the tragic loading of this bed. This is thy work. The object poisons sight. Let it be hid".*

Lodovico, the voice of reason demands the audience and the characters to be aware of how passion can overcome reason and lead to tragedy.

The image of sight and blindness recurs in Shakespeare's plays and highlights the concept seeing should lead to understanding, and not to trust what one hears or be fooled by appearances. A play is a visual medium and it is only through soliloquy the audience is aware of Iago's villainy. Would the audience be duped, like Othello, if Iago's intentions were not made known? .

Section 3.3 Images of Disease and Corruption

The images of disease and corruption are very much used to highlight the strong emotions of love and hate, jealousy and betrayal and the effect of madness is considered in all three of its meanings. Mad can mean angry, obsessed or insane; Othello becomes all three thanks to the machinations of Iago. How emotions can corrupt reason and lead to physical illness is also a major theme highlighted by this imagery.

Iago is well aware the news of Desdemona's marriage to the Moor will cause pain to her father and to Othello. The imagery of disease and corruption of Iago's words reflects this.

> "Poison his delight....plague him with flies",

Iago says with relish and encourages Roderigo to provoke Brabantio's prejudice. Arguably the sickness Brabantio suffers is a form of madness brought about by his disgust with his daughter. Iago tells Othello how Brabantio

> "spoke such scurvy, and provoking terms"

when he heard of the marriage.

Shakespeare often equates falling in love with disease imagery and in *Othello* the relationship between the Moor and Desdemona is highlighted with disease and witchcraft imagery. Brabantio accuses Othello of spellbinding Desdemona

> "with drugs or minerals".

She has become

> "corrupted by spells and medicines of mountebanks"

which are

"powerful o'er the blood".

Love has been brought about by magic and medicine; for how else could a pure, white woman fall in love with an old, black man?

Othello's account of how he wooed Desdemona also highlights the disease of love. It was the *"distressful stroke"* and *"pains"* he suffered that caused Desdemona to pity him and love him for the *"dangers"* he had endured. The duke recognises love as being a *"remedy"* to such *"pains"*, but the duke's decision that Desdemona and Othello's marriage is lawful causes Brabantio a *"bruised heart"* and to be

"pierc'd through the ear".

Brabantio is so distressed it eventually causes his demise.

The *"sick fool, Roderigo,"* is also painfully in love with Desdemona and the marriage provokes him to consider suicide.

"We have a prescription to die, when death is our physician",

he says, but is ridiculed by Iago who believes his *"injury"* is temporary and tells him to overcome his emotions with rationale.

"We have reason to cool our raging motions, our carnal stings, or unbitted lusts",

he states, and, in order to gain favour with Desdemona, Iago urges Roderigo to use his head, saying

"a pox of drowning thyself".

Shakespeare warns his audience of the need to *"love moderately"* in *Romeo and Juliet* and the concept of not allowing the heart to rule the head is reiterated in *Othello*.

Love being a source of madness is highlighted in the story of Barbary who was

> *"in love, and he she loved proved mad"*.

Like Othello, her lover was consumed by suspicion. She fell ill and died, lamenting a lost love. Is it jealousy or love, or both, that send Othello *"into an epilepsy"*?

Emilia considers the *"ills"* of men equate with the *"ills"* of women.

> *"The ills we do, their ills instruct us so"*,

she says, blaming men for teaching women the evils and sins of the world.

"Lust" is viewed as a disease of the flesh, a corruption of the mind. Iago condemns Desdemona of

> *"lechery...lust and foul thoughts"*

and asks Roderigo,

> *"What delight shall she have...when the blood is made dull with the act of sport?"*

His question stresses his supposition that Desdemona will tire of the Moor and lead her to seek Roderigo's passion.

Othello at the end of the play considers the *"bed lust-stain'd"* and with

> *"lust's blood be spotted"*

as he plans to kill his *"disloyal"* wife. Lust is a result of a heightened flow of blood through the body and Shakespeare compares it to a disease. Lust too is quick to overcome reason and send men *"mad"* with passion.

Anger, betrayal and hatred are emotions emphasised by

disease and corruption imagery. The hatred Iago feels towards Othello is seen as a *"poisonous mineral"* that *"gnaws [his] innards"*. Iago warns Roderigo Othello is

> *"rash, and very sudden in choler"*.

This is proven when Othello demotes Cassio, but Othello sees himself as a *"surgeon"* cutting off the opportunity for further fighting.

When Othello has *"proof"* of Desdemona's adultery he decides to *"poison"* her, but is encouraged by Iago to strangle her in the marriage bed,

> *"the bed she has contaminated"*.

Thus Desdemona's betrayal is seen as a disease.

Othello's outburst when he strikes Desdemona in the presence of Lodovico causes the statesman to ask,

> *"Are his wits safe? Is he not light of brain?"*

suggesting Othello is acting irrationally. His madness (anger, insanity and obsessiveness) cause Othello's emotions to overcome his reason. His hatred and jealousy lead him to commit uxoricide.

Othello becomes enraged with Desdemona when she is confused by his accusations of infidelity. He would have preferred the heavens to rain

> *"all kinds of sores and shames"*

upon his head than for him to suffer the torments of his mind and the anger he experiences due to her supposed betrayal. Before he kills her on the marriage bed Desdemona notes,

> *"Your eyes roll so...Why gnaw you so your nether lip? Some bloody passion shakes your very frame"*,

evoking the anger and hatred Othello feels towards her.

The emotion of jealousy is highlighted too by the disease and corruption image, as it is seen to corrupt the body and the soul. Iago plans to put Othello

> "into a jealousy so strong that judgement cannot cure."

He also hopes Othello will be given to *"madness"* (insanity), where his emotion will overcome his reason. He will pour

> "pestilence into his ear"

and corrupt the Othello's love for Desdemona.

Othello's mind becomes diseased as the thoughts of Desdemona's betrayal and his obsessive jealousy make him *"unwell"* and *"mad"* (angry and insane due to his obsession).

> "I have a pain upon my forehead here",

he complains to Desdemona who sympathises,

> "I am very sorry you are not well",

but Iago relishes Othello's ill-health.

> "The Moor already changes with my poison",

he gloats.

In soliloquy Iago gleefully repeats,

> "Work on, my medicine works",

as Othello's turbulent emotions cause him to become physically ill. The Moor laments,

> "Farewell the tranquil mind, farewell content"

and he falls *"into an epilepsy"*, a *"savage madness"*. Consider how people become sick with nerves at times of stress.

Desdemona discusses with Emilia Othello's change of *"humour"*. He suffers from a *"strange unquietness"* and blames the wars in Cyprus to have

"puddled his clear spirit".

Emilia notes *"the Moor's abused"* and tells of how jealousy *"turned"* the wits of Iago

"the seamy side without",

when he suspected her of adultery.

The idea obsessive emotions can bring about ill health is further considered via Cassio and Desdemona. Othello is put to *"ill-thinking"* and into a literal *"fit"* by Iago's manipulation of his obsessive jealous nature. Cassio too is mentally distressed. Despite having been physically hurt in the fight that brings about his demotion, the emotional

"hurt...past all surgery"

is Cassio's loss of *"reputation"*. Desdemona pities Cassio's pains and tells Othello, Cassio

"has left part of his grief with me to suffer with him"

evoking the concept that emotional pain is as damaging as physical pain and can be equally as contagious.

Othello when seeking the truth of Desdemona's treachery takes her hand and believes her physical state reflects her emotional being.

"This hand is moist my Lady",

he observes,

"hot, hot and moist".

Othello sees her damp hand as evidence of her lying about the handkerchief, which she is, but not for the reason Othello suspects.

Finally actual physical harm occurs during the final fight sequence where Roderigo is mortally wounded and Cassio's

"leg cut in two".

Cassio *"faints"* and Iago views the scene as *"bloody"*. The disease imagery highlights the corruption Iago has brought about in Cyprus. The final act of Othello is also bloody as he *"stabs himself"* and Lodovico reflects on how the scene *"poisons my sight"* evoking the corrupt, evil tragedy that has unfolded due to villainous Iago.

Disease and corruption images highlight the emotions of love and hate, jealousy and betrayal and how these emotions can conquer reason, resulting in the physical effects of madness in all three of its forms: anger, obsessiveness and insanity. Excessive emotional reactions can manifest themselves in physical symptoms for which the only cure is reason and moderation. Shakespeare warns of how people can make themselves ill and cause their lives to end in tragedy. He also forces his audience to consider how man can spread a *"poison"* that sends men *"mad"*, thus beware of the judging people by their appearance.

Section 3.4: Images of Clothing

Shakespeare was decidedly interested in how people were judged or, more interestingly, misjudged by their appearance. He played on the audience's expectation the characters would behave in a manner reflecting their dress and demeanour. Much depends on the costume designer, director and the ability of the actors to convey that expectation, which the audience subsequently learns is a mask hiding the true reality of the character's personality. When watching a production consider each of the characters in turn, assessing how they dress and how their clothing is an image to reinforce the themes of appearance versus reality, prejudice, deception and deceit.

Othello should appear as a soldier of high standing, prompting the audience to question why a Moor would appear as such and not as the expected slave or servant. This of course highlights the theme of prejudice, which is enforced by Brabantio who is alarmed his daughter has married a man, whom he believes is inferior to her simply by the colour of his skin. The audience may sympathise with Brabantio, alarmed that

> *"an old black ram is tupping your white ewe"*,

but Othello's clothing should reflect his eloquence when he tells the duke how he wooed Desdemona. He says he will speak *"unbonnetted"*; not hide the truth, reminding the audience not to judge by appearance and clothing can hide a man's true character. People wear different hats!

As the play progresses and Othello allows his emotions to overcome his reason, he may become less well attired, especially when he falls *"into an epilepsy"*. When watching a production, study Othello's costume and see if it reflects a soldier, or a man losing his mind.

Iago warns Roderigo to be aware appearance. He vows to

> *"wear [his] heart upon [his] sleeve"*

suggesting he will be honest with Roderigo, which is ironic, as *"honest Iago"* is far from what he appears to be. Dressed as Othello's ancient, he would be of soldierly bearing and thus expected to have high moral values. Yet Iago warns the audience

> *"I am not what I am."*

Despite his words the audience may still be shocked by Iago's villainy. Iago suggests he will wear two hats, which he does, and his appearance belies his evil villainy. He admits in soliloquy he will

> *"plume up [his hat] in double knavery"*,

a plume being a decoration for a hat often displayed to show a person's status.

He also refers to the *"shows"* men put on and states it is a

> *"divinity of hell, when devils will the blackest sins put on"*,

implying evil is something a man wears or creates himself, it is not something innate.

Ironically, in conversation with Othello, Iago says men

> *"should be what they seem"*

yet instructs Othello how to appear to Desdemona.

> *"Wear your eyes thus: not jealous, nor secure"*,

teaching Othello to dissemble.

Iago is fully cognisant of human beings judging others by appearance and uses the knowledge to weave his *"web"*.

Cassio appears the noble soldier but, once he has lost his

"reputation" he has to appear to be *"content"* with his demotion.

> *"So shall I clothe me in false content"*,

he tells Desdemona. Shakespeare is reminding the audience that people often put on a brave face in times of adversity, an appearance that belies the reality.

Othello accuses Desdemona of appearing *"obedient"* when he believes she has disobeyed her marriage vows.

> *"Oh well painted passion"*,

he spits, as she sobs following his cruelty to her and he strikes her. Ironically, poor Desdemona's act is not an appearance but a genuine reality. Her death wearing a nightgown and on the white sheets of her wedding night, poignantly signifies her purity and innocence on her deathbed.

Desdemona is often dressed in white to reflect her purity and innocence, Emilia being dressed in more plain clothes to imply her pragmatism. Bianca, the prostitute, may appear in apparel more garish, especially scarlet, highlighting her profession.

Brabantio's appearance in his *"night-gown"* reveals to the audience that it is night (enforcing the light and dark image), but it also implies Brabantio's prejudice does not befit a nobleman.

Roderigo is sometimes dressed in expensive clothes to prove his has money. The audience would then expect him to be intelligent and honourable, but would soon learn beneath his display of riches he is a fool and a dupe.

The image of clothing can be lost in a production, but Shakespeare's message is clear. Do not judge by appearance, be wary of putting on an act and be aware all may not be what it seems.

Section 3.5: Images of Food, Appetite and Hunger

The image of food, appetite and hunger stresses the theme of passion and encourages the audience to focus on emotion versus reason, jealousy, love and revenge. Love and loved ones are endearingly referred to as *"sweet"*, and Shakespeare considers how women's appetites are similar to those of men. Overindulgence brings unhappiness and tragedy, whereas repletion brings contentment and stability.

The image of food is very much related simply to women being viewed as a means to sate the lusts of men. Iago tells Roderigo what Desdemona means to Othello. She is

"the food that to him now is as luscious as locusts shall be to him shortly as bitter as coloquintida".

The simile suggests Othello will tire of Desdemona in the same way people tire of even the most delicious food if it is eaten every day.

Emilia explains men

"Are all but stomachs, and we (women) all but food. They eat us hungerly, and when they are full they belch us."

The metaphor is a cynical view of how men use women to fulfil their needs, then cast them aside without a second thought. Yet Shakespeare asks his audience to consider whether women act in a similar manner to men.

Othello realises women, although *"delicate creatures"*, are beings in their own right and men cannot control the *"appetites"* of their women. Such a realisation fuels his jealousy, believing Desdemona has affections for Cassio, which leaves him devastated. Even Emilia points out women have tastes similar to men when she says,

"They see and smell and have their palates for both sweet and

> *sour as husbands have",*

suggesting women are as capable of extreme passions as men.

This neatly introduces the image of appetite. Iago says to Othello,

> *"I see you are eaten up with passion",*

and Shakespeare uses the images of hunger, food and appetite to emphasise the need to satisfy emotions of revenge, jealousy and love. Iago admits he loves Desdemona, not in the same manner as Roderigo or Othello but because she will *"diet my revenge"*. Iago's appetite for revenge needs to be satisfied in the same way a hungry stomach needs to be fed.

Jealousy fuels Othello's existence and becomes a passion that overtakes his reason. Jealousy is

> *"the green-ey'd monster which doth mock the meat it feeds on".*

The metaphor conveys the damage jealousy does to not only the victim but to the perpetrator, eating away at rationale and reason, and this is borne out in the tragedy.

Do not forget Othello's irrational jealousy springs from his overwhelming love for Desdemona, which is also highlighted by the food, hunger and appetite imagery. Othello explains to the duke how he wooed Desdemona at her father's house. She would listen

> *"with a greedy ear"*

and

> *"devour up my discourse",*

evoking how Desdemona was enthralled and enamoured by

the Moor.

Othello's love for Desdemona is so deep he would not be able to fulfil his duties without her and therefore asks the duke's permission for Desdemona to accompany him to Cyprus

> *"to please the palate of [his] appetite"*.

The love shared by Othello and Desdemona is further highlighted by them *"feasting"* on each other.

Following the defeat of the Turkish fleet, Othello feasts with his men and feasts on Desdemona in the marital bed. He asks Desdemona to accompany him to bed where

> *"the fruits are to ensue"*.

The concept of fruit conveys fecundity and Desdemona's appearance is later referred to as *"fruitful"*. In Shakespeare's time women were considered attractive if they were able to bear children.

The act of sexual intercourse with a woman satisfies the *"appetite"* yet, too much congress with a woman (or a man) can also

> *"begin to heave the gorge, disrelish"*

the act of love. Too much of a good thing becomes ordinary, distasteful or worthless.

Desdemona's love for Othello is described by Iago as an *"appetite"* as he realises he can make Othello jealous, thus using their affection for each other to bring about the Moor's downfall. The act of sexual intercourse is often in Shakespeare shrouded with reference to the consumption of food and symbolically sex is seen as the seductive ingestion of grapes, strawberries and wine.

Love and loved ones are also viewed as *"sweet"*, a taste that brings delight and pleasure. Cassio refers to *"Sweet Bianca"* and Desdemona calls her husband *"Sweet Othello"*, an endearment to show how much she loves him. Othello frequently refers to Desdemona as *"my Sweet"*, *"Sweet lady"* and *"Sweeting"* highlighting his desire for her. In contrast, Iago refers to Othello as a *"bless'd pudding"* suggesting *"Sweet Desdemona"* has made a fool of him and love has unhinged him.

It is overindulgence that brings the downfall of Othello. As he *"loved too much"* his passion clouded his reason. Emilia scorns Othello as being worse than

"a beggar in his drink"

having killed his wife suggesting Othello's passions have made him drunk or irrational. Similarly Cassio's overindulgence on wine brings about his downfall. Although Cassio laments,

"courtesy would invent some other custom of entertainment".

He drinks the wine offered to him and subsequently loses his reason.

"O God, that men should put an enemy in their mouths",

he cries, having been demoted and the *"invisible spirit"* is seen as an *"ingredient"* of the devil.

In contrast to overindulgence is the concept of repletion, which brings feelings of wellbeing and contentment. Othello states he was

"fed well, was free and merry"

and had *"sweet sleep"* prior to his suspicions of Desdemona's infidelity.

Brabantio is enraged when

"being full of supper, and distemp'ring draughts"

he hears news of his daughter's marriage to Othello. Being well fed is associated with being in good health and good humour. In order Othello look more kindly on Cassio, following his demotion, Desdemona states that she will ensure her husband will

"feed on nourishing dishes"

and Othello finds Desdemona attractive because she *"feeds well"* and has a *"sweet body"*, suggesting she pleases his taste in women.

The image of food, appetite and hunger fortifies the themes of emotion versus reason, jealousy, love and revenge. Sexual congress and attraction is seen as fruitful and sweet; women and men both having similar appetites. Repletion brings contentment and stability, yet overindulgence brings unhappiness and tragedy, confirming the adage: 'too much of a good thing is bad for you'.

Section 3.6: Images of Heaven and Hell, Demons and Monsters, Fate and Fortune

Heaven and Hell

In its most simplistic form heaven is the residence of the gods, hell of devils. Heaven is where a good person goes following his death; hell is a place of punishment for bad people. Shakespeare uses images of heaven and hell to convey the major theme of good and evil, however, in *Othello* good and evil are not separate concepts, but are entwined. Good people can do evil, evil people can do good; ergo people are both good and evil. The two are not mutually exclusive but are often in conflict.

Hell is evoked as being a place of pain. Iago states he hates Othello

"as I do hell pains",

suggesting Iago's enraged feelings towards Othello are agonising. Iago further alludes to Othello as being a source of pain, associating his skin colour with hell, and urges Brabantio to hurry lest

"the devil make a grandsire of you"

depicting Othello as a devil and conveying the pain Brabantio will suffer if he condones the marriage of Desdemona to Othello.

As Othello becomes insanely jealous, Iago notes his poison burns

"like the mines of sulphur".

The image of the torment of hell is further conveyed by Othello himself. *"Horrors accumulate"*, he wails and portrays the heavens weeping, and thoughts of *"damnation"*. Believing he has proof of Cassio philandering with his wife, Othello cries,

"Arise black vengeance from the hollow hell".

In many of Shakespeare's plays vengeance ends in tragedy and is viewed as hellish. Yet Othello also says,

"tis the spite of hell, the Fiend's arch-mock, to lip a wanton in a secure couch and suppose her chaste",

meaning the devil is toying with him, making Desdemona appear virtuous. Othello believes he is a victim of the devil, whereas he is a victim of the mortal Iago.

In soliloquy Iago plots to ruin Cassio and Othello and concludes his speech with the rhyming couplet,

"Hell and night must bring this monstrous birth to the world's light".

The images of darkness, hell and monsters vividly convey his evil intentions. Where Iago is equated with devils, monsters and hell, Desdemona is surrounded by heavenly imagery to highlight her beauty and virtue. Cassio alliteratively calls her *"divine Desdemona"* and asks for

"the Grace of Heaven' keep her safe".

Desdemona's language is full of references to her faith: she often talks about heaven.

"Lord have mercy on me...By heaven you do me wrong...O heaven forgive us",

Desdemona cries, having been accused of adultery by her husband.

"Heaven have mercy on me",

Desdemona pleads before Othello smothers her and finally Emilia sums up Desdemona's and Othello's personalities with the paradox,

"O, the more angel she, and you the blacker devil".

Images of hell and damnation recur in *Othello*, especially towards the end of the play, when Othello becomes preoccupied with the religious and moral judgement of Desdemona and himself. Othello initially derides Desdemona as a *"devil"* when he believes her to be cheating him and calls for her to be *"damned"*. Paradoxically, on her deathbed, he relents wishing for her to die in a State of Grace. He asks if she has prayed that night as he

"would not kill [her] unprepared spirit".

He wishes for her to go to heaven despite his belief she has betrayed him.

Conflict of good and evil (heaven and hell)
Heaven and hell being in conflict is present in the play to show how good men can easily succumb to evil, and how evil men can portray an appearance of goodness.

Cassio's demotion is due to his own foolishness in drinking with Iago. He is a 'good' character but when drunk he becomes violent, therefore 'bad'. Cassio announces

"God's above all...God forgive us our sins",

but it is not God who brings about Cassio's loss of *"reputation"*. God may forgive Cassio's foolishness, but Cassio cannot forgive himself. He even refers to the drink as an *"unblessed", "invisible spirit"* of the *"devil"* that makes men succumb

"to the devil wrath".

The appearance and reality theme is particularly pertinent to Iago who, knows he is evil but puts on a *"show"* of being *"honest"*.

"Divinity of hell, when devils will the blackest sins put on, they

do suggest at first with heavenly shows, as I do now".

Later Iago conveys how he will dupe Othello by pouring

"pestilence into his ear"

but retain the appearance of *"honest Iago".*

Another good example of the conflict of heaven and hell, good versus evil, is when Othello believes Desdemona is deceiving him. He claims,

"Heaven truly knows that thou art false as hell".

The concept heaven knows the truth is alluded to several times: Desdemona on her deathbed claims, *"Heaven doth know"* the truth of her actions, but she is cruelly murdered by her obsessive husband who has been fooled by the *"demi-devil",* Iago. The conflict between good versus evil in *Othello* ends in tragedy, with both Cassio and Iago (good and evil) still remaining, suggesting good and evil still exist in the world today. Neither can easily be recognised until it is too late.

Images of demons and monsters
The images of demons and monsters highlight the themes of jealousy, betrayal and emotion versus reason.

In order to induce Othello to jealousy Iago manipulates conversation about Cassio and Desdemona by repeating Othello's words. Othello counterattacks,

"He echoes me as if there were some monster in his thought"

which is ironic considering Iago's thoughts are indeed monstrous. He is determined to make Othello jealous, a destructively fiendish emotion.

With twisted irony, Iago tells Othello to beware of jealousy, the

> "green-ey'd monster which doth mock the meat it feeds on",

evoking the avarice of jealousy. Likewise, Emilia describes jealousy as dangerously and uncannily self-generating,

> "a monster begot upon itself, born on itself".

Having become jealous Othello sees his existence as monstrous.

> "Oh monstrous world...monstrous, monstrous!"

he cries with images of hell

> "fire and suffocating streams".

Shakespeare, via monster and hell imagery, conveys his belief that jealousy is destructive and all-consuming.

The sin of adultery (refer to the Seventh Commandment) and uxoricide (the Sixth Commandment) are actions condemned as demonic. Othello views Desdemona's betrayal as *"monstrous, monstrous!"* and in the final act he damns himself to hell for the murder of his wife with the words,

> "Hurl my soul from Heaven and fiends will snatch at it...Whip me, ye devils . . . roast me in sulphur, wash me in steep-down gulfs of liquid fire!"

Othello reasons he deserves eternal spiritual and physical torture in hell as punishment for murder, but Shakespeare is asking his audience what punishment should be meted out. Is a husband permitted to kill his wife for adultery? Is Othello to be pitied considering he is in such agony and his emotions have overcome his reason? Is this reason for clemency? Is Othello too severe on himself?

In conjunction with the appearance versus reality theme consider how the images of monsters, devils and damnation are used to describe the characters. Iago's evilness is particularly portrayed by devilish and monster imagery. At the end of the play, following the denouement, Montano claims Iago's machinations as a *"monstrous act"* which is accompanied by devil imagery. Iago is branded a *"devil"*, *"a demon"*, a *"demi-devil"*, a *"damned villain"* and a *"pernicious...hellish villain"*. The epithets are deserved considering his treacherous nature.

In contrast Iago's opinion of others is similar. He believes Othello to be a *"devil"* and Cassio *"a devilish knave"*. Othello too condemns Desdemona as a *"devil"* and to be *"damned"* when he finds proof of her alleged adultery. This derogatory name-calling belies the truthful personalities of these characters.

The imagery of the monstrous and diabolical takes over where the imagery of animals can go no further, presenting the jealous-crazed characters not simply as brutish, but as deformed and demonic.

<u>Looking to the heavens for guidance and protection</u>
Characters call upon the heavens to help them or to care for others. Othello calls upon the Heavens to

"defend your good souls"

when the duke and the senate decide Othello be accompanied by his bride to Cyprus. Montano hopes Othello survives the storm on his way to Cyprus agreeing Othello be safe with the words,

"Pray Heavens he be".

and Cassio asks,

"Oh let the Heavens give him defence against the elements".

Desdemona begs,

"the Heavens forbid but that our loves and comforts should increase even as our days do grow".

Lodovico states,

> "God save you worthy General",

when he witnesses Othello's anger with Desdemona.

Enraged, having been let down by Cassio, Othello seeks guidance from the gods.

> "Now by Heaven, my blood begins my safer guides to rule"

he says and promptly demotes his lieutenant. Today people look to God (even the non-believers) for assistance by offering up prayers such as 'God help me!' or 'Thank God'.

Exclamation of passions and veracity
Reference to the gods is also used to denote exclamations of passion. *"Great Jove!"* Cassio states on the arrival of Desdemona to Cyprus pleased to see she is safe.

In the same way people today show sincerity by stating 'Honest to God', the characters in *Othello* also swear their veracity by vowing to heaven. In soliloquy Iago avers,

> "As Heaven is my judge, not I for love or duty"

swearing he is not a loving or duteous man. In this context Iago's words are truthful but, ironically, much of what Iago says is false and manipulative.

In times of adversity characters look to higher beings for assistance, to prove honesty and show passion. Shakespeare proves that taking an oath is easily broken and a man's word is not always his bond.

Fate and Fortune
The question of freewill arises in many of Shakespeare's plays. Othello rhetorically asks,

> "Who can control his Fate?"

a query still debated today. Is mankind at the mercy of gods presiding in heaven, toying with lives or do people have freedom of choice and bring about their own fate or fortune by their own decisions? Typically Shakespeare does not (nor cannot) answer the question, but leaves his audience to ponder the concept of freewill. What is shown however is actions do have consequences.

Fortune is the tool by which the gods show favour and is often personified in Shakespeare using a capital 'F'. Othello believes fortune has shone upon him in bringing him the love of Desdemona and the Duke of Venice agrees *"Fortune"* has taken Desdemona and placed her in the arms of Othello. Desdemona too sees it as good fortune to be Othello's wife.

When Othello falls into a *"trance"* believing he has proof of Desdemona's adultery, Iago asks Othello to

>*"bear [his] fortune like a man"*,

conveying the concept that men should endure what the gods mete out and overcome it. Desdemona laments her *"wretched fortune"* on her deathbed, which is most poignant and tragic because she is an innocent victim.

Fate is the other tool used by the gods to bring about events and it is Iago who uses Fate as a tool himself. He tells Othello he overheard Cassio in sleep *"bemoan his Fate"* that Desdemona was given to Othello and not to him.

Shakespeare however makes his audience consider whether Fate and Fortune are in the hands of the gods or in the hands of men. Iago sarcastically savours Othello's ruination stating,

>*"He knows not yet of his honourable fortune"*

as he plots with Roderigo. Othello's demise is through Iago's machinations, not those of gods or devils.

A good example of the paradox of divine intervention versus freewill is when Emilia claims she found the handkerchief by *"fortune"*, but she decides to give it to her husband with the words,

> *"What he will do with it, Heaven knows, not I"*

as if her action becomes a decision of the gods. Of course, it is Iago's choice to use it to bring about the downfall of Othello.

The stars and planets were believed to have an influence on the actions of men and a tool of the gods to decide man's destiny. Iago explains to Othello, following the brawl resulting in Cassio's demotion, that it was

> *"as if some planet had unwitted men"*

suggesting the zodiac was responsible for rowdy behaviour and not the men themselves. Consider today how people still consult their horoscopes, the tarot cards and birth charts to influence their lives.

Othello claims the *"Moon winks"* at him when Desdemona genuinely asks what sin she has committed. The moon is associated with lunacy and Shakespeare's reference here is the moon is mocking Othello.

Later Othello blames the movements of the moon for making him *"mad"* yet, once again, Shakespeare makes his audience consider whether Othello's actions are due to heavenly intervention or through his own. In the final moments of his life Othello takes responsibility for his failings. Following Desdemona's death Othello believes there should be a divine sign,

> *"a huge eclipse of Sun and Moon"*.

Ironically a momentous event does occur: the revelation of Desdemona's innocence and Iago's treachery.

Regardless of freewill or divine control, Shakespeare's play shows all actions have consequences for which men must be held accountable. Did God give people freewill in order that they take responsibility for their lives?

Conclusion

The images of heaven, hell, devils and monsters highlight the themes of good and evil, appearance versus reality, emotion versus reason, jealousy, revenge and betrayal. They also highlight the actions and personalities of the characters and raise questions with regard to choice and control. The repeated use of these images forces Shakespeare's audience to think about their own lives, choices and personalities and this is why Shakespeare is still studied today.

Section 3.7: Natural Imagery

Images associated with nature recur frequently in *Othello* to emphasise themes and character traits; to build up tension and create atmosphere, bringing the play vividly to life. Remember Shakespeare was not expecting his audience to read the plays, but to see them, thus images allow the audience to notice recurring concepts in *Othello*.

Images of Plants
Plants are used to emphasise power and control, to highlight the themes of emotion versus reason, love and poisonous revenge.

Iago is strangely preoccupied with plants. His speeches to Roderigo in particular make extensive and elaborate use of vegetable metaphors. The tending of a garden highlights the emotion versus reason theme. Just as people tend a garden so should they tend their emotions.

> *"Our bodies are our gardens, to which our wills are gardeners; so that if we will plant nettles or sow lettuce, set hyssop and weed up thyme...the power and corrigible authority of this lies in our wills".*

Iago explains people have the power to do good or evil and the choice of which to do. Iago, according to his own metaphor, is a good *"gardener"*. He has the ability to will or manipulate others in the same way a gardener can encourage a plant to grow in a certain manner. Shakespeare implies man has freewill to decide his own fate, which is paradoxical to predetermination, when the gods or God control man's destiny.

Iago also uses botanical imagery to explain those who act swiftly will reap the benefits. He says to Roderigo encouraging him to continue his pursuit of Desdemona,

> *"Though other things grow fair against the sun, Yet fruits that blossom first will first be ripe".*

If Roderigo acts quickly he will win the love of Desdemona.

Many of Iago's botanical references concern poison, which neatly reflects Iago's evil character. He relishes his plan suggesting to Othello that Desdemona has been unfaithful with Cassio.

> *"I'll pour this pestilence into his ear",*

he says and later gloats,

> *"The Moor already changes with my poison. Dangerous conceits are in their natures poisons...not poppy nor mandragora nor all the drowsy syrups of the world shall ever medicine thee to that sweet sleep".*

Iago is delighted Othello is troubled by his suspicions and is losing sleep and his good health.

Iago cultivates his *"syrups"* so they become lethal poisons and then plants their seeds in the minds of others. His plotting, via botanic metaphors, makes his evil conniving seem like a force of nature. The metaphor also indicates the mind of the other characters is fertile ground for his efforts.

Natural imagery is used in Shakespeare to highlight the theme of love. When Othello is explaining how he wooed Desdemona he speaks of

> *"flood and field ... rough quarries, rocks, hills"*

and, accompanied with heavenly images, the speech evokes Othello's deep love for Desdemona.

The song *"Willow"* is a love song featuring betrayal, wherein the woman in the song is betrayed by her lover. Emilia dies singing the song but ironically it is Emilia who betrays her husband, albeit by revealing the truth. The song's lyrics suggest both men and women are unfaithful to one another, thus highlighting Othello's belief in Desdemona's adultery.

To Desdemona, the song seems to represent acceptance of her alienation from Othello's affections, and singing it leads her to question Emilia about the nature and practice of infidelity. The natural image conveys that love, like a weeping willow, ends in tears.

Images of plants are depicted on Desdemona's deathbed. Othello refers to trees and to Desdemona as a *"rose"*, a flower symbolic of love, but it has its thorns!

Animal Imagery
In Shakespeare animal imagery is used to highlight character traits, used as insults and to reveal the time of day.

Before the audience even sees Othello, Iago and Roderigo describe him in a prejudicial derogatory manner. In the Venetian imagination, Othello's power resides in his sexual difference from white males. Iago prejudicially connects Othello's ethnicity with bestiality.

"An old black ram is tupping your white ewe",

Iago calls to Brabantio, adding,

"Your daughter and the Moor are now making the beast with two backs".

and

"you'll have your daughter covered with a Barbary horse...you'll have your nephews neigh to you; you'll have coursers for cousins and jennets for germans".

(A *"jennet"* is a small Spanish horse or female donkey, *"coursers"* are racehorses and the word *"germans"* means close blood relatives.)

In Art horses are symbolic of sexual power and the early scenes of the play are full of images and anxieties of Othello's sexuality contrasted with a Venetian woman's purity. The picture depicted by Iago enrages Brabantio's (and possibly the audience's) prejudices without having seen Othello. The Jacobean audience would expect a savage Moor, but Othello is not *"savage"*, he loves and reveres Desdemona. Shakespeare cleverly shows one shouldn't believe everything one hears, nor should prejudice bias opinions of individuals. How Othello appears in Iago's insults is far from the reality.

In *Othello* Shakespeare's view of mankind is somewhat low and contemptible. He uses animal imagery to reduce men and their actions to that of beasts. Iago comments,

> *"There's many a beast in a populous city and many a civil monster"*,

thereby warning the audience men can be bestial, especially when they lose their reason.

Iago explains to Roderigo that he is *"silly"* to lament over Desdemona's marriage to Othello. Roderigo should not speak of drowning himself as Iago points out Othello will tire of Desdemona. Iago tells Roderigo,

> *"Ere I would say I would drown myself for the love of a guinea-hen, I would change my humanity with a baboon"*

meaning that he would rather be a monkey than kill himself over a woman. He then remarks, drowning is for

> *"cats and blind puppies"*,

suggesting Roderigo's talk of suicide, because he has lost his *"love"*, is infantile. Iago uses the derisory *"guinea-hen"*, a euphemism for a prostitute to describe women, and later refers to them as *"wildcats"* which gives an indication of his low opinion of womankind.

In the same way Iago, if he becomes irrational, wishes to be transformed into a baboon, Othello tells Iago,

> "Exchange me for a goat when I shall turn the business of my soul to such exsufflicate and blowed surmises",

meaning he should become a goat rather than listen to lies and become jealous. The demand is ironic as Iago's falsehoods and contrived scenarios lead to Othello's irrational jealousy. The frequent references to goats and monkeys suggest allegedly lascivious creatures. When Othello is forced to leave Cyprus he spits,

> "You are welcome Sir to Cyprus. Goats and monkeys",

evoking his anger at Lodovico's decision Cassio take his place. Cyprus is thus demoted to bestial status, and it is certainly the setting where Othello's behaviour sinks to a bestial level.

Rather than enduring the humiliation of a cuckold, Othello says he would prefer to be a

> "toad and live upon the vapour of a dungeon, than keep a corner in the thing I love for others' uses".

The inference is men, betrayed by women, have little respect and control over their household. Such men Othello believes are low creatures indeed.

Othello laments Desdemona's alleged dishonesty comparing her actions to

> "summer flies...in the shambles, that quicken even with blowing".

The image is of flies breeding rapidly around butcher's shops, an insult comparable to the heavenly images surrounding Desdemona.

Emilia, in her final moments, says she will

> "play the swan and die in music",

suggesting she will die a contented death having served her purpose to expose her husband's treachery.

The repeated references to animals convey a sense that the laws of nature, rather than those of society, are the primary forces governing the characters in this play. Consider how Iago is sure

> *"[Othello] will be as tenderly led by the nose as asses are"*.

Even though mankind is governed by civilised rule and etiquette, man has the capability of reverting to bestial behaviour once reason is lost and emotions enraged.

Similarly animal imagery is used to show disgust at the drunken behaviour of people, who once intoxicated lose their reason and therefore their civility. Iago has a low opinion of his fellow soldiers. Whilst they celebrate he refers to them as a *"flock of drunkards"* and when drunk Cassio laments he is

> *"by and by a fool, and presently a beast!"*

Having lost his *"reputation"* what *"remains is bestial"* suggesting a man who loses respect and self-control is nothing more than an animal. The ability to reason raises the human race above many species.

Animal imagery is used, as it is today, to demean a person by deriding them. Characters are referred to as dogs, equated with sexual deviancy and under the control of man.

Roderigo calls Iago *"O inhuman dog!"* and Othello calls Cassio a *"dog"* when he believes Cassio is bragging of his dalliance with Desdemona, when really it is Bianca. Lodovico calls Iago *"O, Spartan dog"*, notoriously fierce animals, thus evoking Iago's ferocity in his pursuit of Othello and Cassio's demise. Lodovico also calls Iago a *"viper"* conveying Iago's poisonous nature. Although the term *"dog"* is no longer fashionable, do not forget the more contemporary use of the profanity 'bitch'.

Web imagery and means of trapping animals recurs in the play, specifically surrounding Iago as he manipulates Roderigo and Othello. In order to ensnare Othello, Iago, in soliloquy, plans to turn Desdemona's

> "virtue into pitch and...make the net that shall enmesh them all".

By blackening Desdemona's *"virtue"* Iago knows he will bring down Cassio and Othello. He gloats,

> "with as little a web as this will I ensnare as great a fly as Cassio".

Later he says,

> "indeed my invention comes from my pate as birdlime does from frieze".

Lime was put on the branches of trees where it would stick to birds' feet, thereby trapping them. Entrapment is Iago's skill and is highlighted by animal imagery.

Paradoxically, Shakespeare alludes to entrapment being part of the process of love. Othello sees the handkerchief as a means to entrap Desdemona. He tells her,

> "there is magic in the web of it"

and *"the worms"* from where the silk originated were *"hallow'd"*. Natural imagery surrounds the love theme, but the suggestion is that love is a means by which men and women can manipulate and control others.

Storm Imagery

The storm imagery depicts turmoil both literally and metaphorically in Cyprus and in the actions of the characters. It emphasises tempestuous times, war and emotions. Note the storm is a means by which, people believed, the gods showed their presence or their disapproval, thus it is related to the imagery of heaven and hell.

As Montano and gentlemen wait for news of Othello's fleet, Montano describes a storm has

> *"ruffian'd so upon the sea, what ribs of oak, when the mountains melt on them".*

A gentleman goes on to speak of the

> *"chidden billow seems to pelt the clouds, the wind-shak'd surge"*

and alongside *"monstrous"* imagery Shakespeare creates tension, forcing the audience to be concerned for Othello and Desdemona. Cassio then brings news of how *"divine Desdemona"* and Othello have survived the *"tempest"* suggesting they have deified status capable of calming the storm. Othello remarks, following a storm there is calm, which to the audience would suggest a prediction of godlike capability. Othello's status as a competent leader is assured.

Storm imagery is used in the unmasking of Iago's treachery.

> *"What serves for the thunder?"*

Othello asks, bewildered as to why Iago has gone to such lengths to bring about his ruination. The image serves to act as an evil backdrop to the tragedy.

Storm imagery denotes turmoil. Iago's evil nature brings about turmoil in the lives of those under Othello's authority in Cyprus. On stage the storm maybe accompanied by music or conveyed by percussion instruments, but do not forget, even today, in many productions evil acts take place during a storm in order to create tension and instil fear into the audience. In the 16th and 17th centuries thunderstorms were greatly feared by the people and seen as the wrath of God, which adds to their ferocity.

Section 3.8: Images of Magic and Witchcraft

Witches, magic, sorcery and warlocks were a part of seventeenth century life. Coincidence, the unexplained, the root of fears could be blamed on the magical and on those who had magical powers. In the play *Othello*, Shakespeare asks his audience to consider the unexplained does not involve magic, but simply the actions of men themselves.

Brabantio accuses Othello of using *"charms...spells"* and

> *"magic to 'enchant [his] daughter"*.

It is Brabantio's belief *"witchcraft"* is at work as, he cannot envisage his daughter falling in love with a black man of her own accord. Othello refutes these claims explaining he wooed Desdemona with *"words"*. She felt *"pity"* for the *"dangers"* he had faced and he loved her because of her *"pity"*. Their love sprang from his visits to Brabantio's house and subsequent conversations and feelings, not via *"witchcraft"*.

> *"We know we work by wit and not by witchcraft"*,

Iago alliteratively tells Roderigo, when Roderigo is ready to forsake his pursuit of Desdemona. Indeed, Iago works via his wits, playing Roderigo for a fool, manipulating Othello into a jealous rage, using Emilia to assist in his machinations to bring about Othello and Cassio's ruination, deceiving others of his villainy. Iago is the character who proves to the audience magic, witchcraft and spells do not bring about evil, men do that themselves.

The handkerchief is a red herring on which the audience could base their beliefs that any one who touches the handkerchief becomes blighted by jealousy. Othello claims it was made by a *"charmer"* who could

> *"almost read the thoughts of people"*,

but the handkerchief does not cause Othello to become jealous, it is merely a piece of cloth, a tool, used by Iago to prove (falsely) that Desdemona and Cassio are lovers. Bianca is deceived by the presence of the handkerchief in Cassio's chamber and Desdemona herself sees it as *"a wonder"*, almost believing it has magical powers.

The power of suggestion is used by Iago, not the power of magic. Iago suggests Desdemona is unfaithful with Cassio and orchestrates acts that seem to confirm her adultery. Othello believes Iago, because he mistakenly knows him to be *"honest"*. It is the emotions of men that brings about their downfall; their own actions bring about ruination, not spells, nor charms, nor *"witchcraft"*. Iago claims men work by *"wit"*, and it is when they are *"witless"* they are prone to tragedy.

Section 3. 9 The Handkerchief

The handkerchief symbolises different things to different characters, but brings to the fore concepts of magic, jealousy, influence and love.

Since the handkerchief was the *"first gift"* Desdemona received from Othello, she keeps it about her constantly as a symbol of his love. She values it greater than money.

> *"I had rather have lost my purse full of crusadoes",*

she tells Emilia, as she searches for the handkerchief Emilia has given to her husband out of duty.

Iago manipulates the handkerchief so that Othello comes to see it as a symbol of Desdemona herself, her faith and chastity. By taking possession of it, he is able to convert it into evidence of her infidelity.

But the handkerchief's importance to Iago and Desdemona derives from its importance to Othello himself. He tells Desdemona it was woven by a two hundred-year-old *"Sibyl"*, or female prophet, using silk from sacred worms and dye extracted from the hearts of mummified virgins.

> *"There's magic in the web of it",*

Othello claims, stating his mother used it to keep his father faithful to her. The handkerchief represents, to Othello, marital fidelity. The pattern of strawberries (dyed with virgins' blood) on a white background strongly suggests the bloodstains left on the sheets on a virgin's wedding night, so the handkerchief implicitly suggests a guarantee of virginity as well as fidelity. Strawberries are also fruits symbolic of love as they are heart shaped. The red colour is also a reminder of sexuality.

Desdemona, when seeing Othello's jealousy for the first time, believes the handkerchief is magical.

> *"There's some wonder in the handkerchief",*

she says. This is reiterated later when Bianca is beset by jealousy, and confronts Cassio, accusing it of being

> *"some token from a newer friend".*

Bianca is given the handkerchief by Cassio, who finds it in his chamber, having been placed there by Iago. She views it as *"some minx's token"* and hurls the handkerchief back at Cassio in front of Othello who immediately sees it as proof of Cassio's dalliance with his wife.

The handkerchief does seem to bring about jealousy, but Shakespeare is asking the audience to consider whether it is the supposed magical handkerchief that is making the characters jealous or whether it is indeed of their own doing. In the final scenes, as the truth is revealed and Emilia admits she gave the handkerchief to her husband, the audience is forced to face the truth that the handkerchief is not jinxed, nor magical, but a merely a piece of cloth by which Iago orchestrated his revenge on the Moor.

Section Four: Soliloquies

A soliloquy is when a character speaks at length to his or herself. In Shakespeare's plays when a character delivers a soliloquy it is acknowledged the character speaks from the heart and is telling the absolute truth. This dramatic device allows the audience to be privy to information and thoughts unbeknown to other characters and, more often than not, reveals aspects of the speaker's personality or his or her intent.

Soliloquies prove Shakespeare is a poet as well as a playwright. He uses standard literary devices, repeated images and they prove to be the more colourful aspects of his writing.

Section 4.1: Introduction to Iago's Soliloquies

Some of the following soliloquies may be viewed as asides, but I have chosen to include them as they all convey Iago's twisted evil, using wonderful imagery and turn of phrase.

Why did Shakespeare choose to allow his audience a glimpse into the machinations of Iago's mind? Was it to make Desdemona and Othello's fate more pitiful? Is it to highlight how the most noble and intelligent of men can be duped by the outward appearance of another? Consider how Othello, Desdemona and Cassio believe Iago to be *"honest"*. Does the audience knowing Iago's evil intent add tension to the play? Does being privy to Iago's plans, then see them unfold, make the play more dramatic?

Consider carefully the questions I pose and watch the actor's interpretation of the *"demi-devil"* as he spins his *"web"*.

Section 4.2: Iago's First Soliloquy

"Thus do I ever make my fool my purse...
Must bring this monstrous birth to the world's light."

At the end of Act I Iago delivers his first soliloquy, revealing he only spends time with *"snipes"* (idiots) such as Roderigo to make money or gain an advantage for himself.

He then states,

"I hate the Moor,"

because he suspects Othello has bedded his wife.

"'twixt my sheets
He's done my office,"

he claims, then gloats it is advantageous Othello

"holds me well. The better shall my purpose work on him."

He knows Othello thinks him to be *"honest"* and he will use Othello's good opinion of him to bring about the ruination of the Moor.

Admitting Cassio is *"a proper man"*, Iago plots how

"to get his place."

Repeating, *"How? How?"* the cunning ancient comes up with a plan to *"abuse Othello's ear"* with the lie that Cassio

"is too familiar with his wife."

Iago is fully aware of Othello's

"free and open nature"

thus he can

> *"be led by the nose like asses are."*

The simile suggests Othello to be a fool and nothing more than a simple beast.

Concluding the soliloquy with a rhyming couplet filled with heaven and hell imagery, Iago relishes the prospect of bringing Cassio and Desdemona's supposed affair to the attention of Othello.

> *"Hell and night*
> *Must bring this monstrous birth to the world's light."*

Even Iago himself admits his plan is *"monstrous"* and evil.

In this soliloquy Iago cleverly finds aspects of Othello's personality to use to his own advantage. Iago's talent in reading others accurately is made to serve negative rather than positive purposes. His evil plan sets the scene for the action to come. The first act concludes with the audience wondering *"how"* he will fulfil his purpose.

Section 4.3: Iago's Second Soliloquy

"That Cassio loves her...
...Knavery's plain face is never still seen used."

Iago has witnessed Cassio greeting Desdemona on their arrival in Cyprus. He deduces *"Cassio loves her"*, but is the word love synonymous with respect, not romantic love? It doesn't matter. The fact the two show friendly affection for each other will be to Iago's *"credit"*.

However, he is concerned because he feels Othello will

"prove to Desdemona a most dear husband",

thus the likelihood of Desdemona being unfaithful is diminished.

Iago admits,

"I do love her too"

though his *"love"* for Othello's wife is because she will *"diet"* his *"revenge"* and be the means to bring about Othello's ruin.

He repeats his suspicion the *"lusty Moor"* has slept with his wife,

"leaped into my seat"

and the

"thought ...like a poisonous mineral"

eats away at him. He must therefore have his revenge *"wife for wife"*.

If he cannot do that, he will

*"Put the Moor into a jealousy so strong
That judgement cannot cure."*

Iago, once again, is fully aware of Othello's weakness and will exploit it.

The audience then becomes aware Iago suspects Cassio of having slept with Emilia.

"For I fear Cassio with my nightcap too",

and Iago will *"abuse"* him by telling Othello lies.

Iago admits his plan is still somewhat *"confused"* but evil is not plainly seen until it is enacted.

In this soliloquy Iago is set on *"revenge"* and speaks insultingly of Othello via animal imagery. He maligns women too, believing his wife to have slept with two men. Iago may not have worked out the details of his plan, but his evil is fully premeditated. He knows it is poisonous and he is confident he can take advantage of whatever opportunity comes his way.

Section 4.4: Iago's Third Soliloquy

"If I can fasten but one cup on him
My boat sails freely, both with wind and steam."

Iago lets the audience know of his plan to bring about Cassio's downfall. He hopes to encourage the soldier to drink *"one cup"* more than he should, to make him

"full of quarrel and offence as my young mistress's dog".

He then laughingly explains Roderigo, whose love for Desdemona has turned him

"the wrong side out",

has spent the evening *"carousing"* (drinking) and is to go on guard duty. Furthermore, he has made other guards drunk with *"flowing cups"*, thus all he has to do now is

"put our Cassio in some action that may offend the isle."

He concludes, if *"consequence"* works in his favour, he will happily succeed in ruining Cassio.

In this soliloquy it is revealed how Iago's mind works. He uses the knowledge of Cassio not being able to hold his liquor and Roderigo's infatuation with Desdemona to his advantage. He has put in place a plan to devise a brawl between Roderigo and Cassio, but is aware he hasn't absolute control over consequences. His evil is compounded because he doesn't care about the chances of collateral damage.

Section 4.5: Iago's Fourth Soliloquy

"And what is he then that says I play the villain?...
And out of her own goodness make the net
That shall enmesh them all."

In Act II Scene III Iago wonderfully justifies his actions, almost praising himself as he brings about the ruin of Cassio and Othello.

Following Cassio's demotion Iago tells Cassio to ask Desdemona to speak to her husband.

"Importune her help to put you in your place again,"

he suggests and in this soliloquy Iago begins with a rhetorical question.

"And what's he then that says I play the villain,
When this advice I give is free and honest,
Probal to thinking, and indeed the course to win the Moor again?"

He justifies the advice he has given to Cassio to be *"free and honest"*, but is it? He knows Cassio believes he is *"honest"*, but is Iago's intention *"honest"*? Perhaps speaking to Desdemona may help Cassio's *"suit"*, as Iago has noted Othello loves her deeply and will do anything for her.

"His soul is so enfettered to her love
That she may make, unmake, do what she list",

and, if said by any other man, the advice could be good *"counsel"*. If Othello does everything Desdemona asks of him, then maybe he would reinstate Cassio.

Iago asks again,

"How am I a villain?"

Once more he justifies his *"advice"* to Cassio as being *"good"*, but is he laughing at his cunning? What is the intent behind this advice?

Iago confesses he is putting on an act. He considers himself a *"devil"*, as he is committing the *"blackest sins"*. He is pretending to be Cassio's confidante and friend but, viewing the man as a *"fool"*, he is actually doing him great harm.

Whilst Cassio is pleading with Desdemona

"to repair his fortunes",

Iago will pour *"pestilence"* into the *"ear"* of Othello.

Iago's intent is poisonous. He will suggest to the Moor that Desdemona's pleadings for Cassio's reinstatement are evidence of her *"lust"* for him. While Desdemona thinks she is doing *"good"*, Iago will ensure her words and *"virtue"* are turned *"into pitch"*. Her pleas will

"undo her credit with the Moor".

Exulting in his machinations, Iago concludes Desdemona's *"goodness"* will

*"make the net
That shall enmesh them all."*

This soliloquy is a wonderful insight into Iago's warped mind. He knows he is a *"devil"*. He knows he is committing the worst of *"sins"* by putting on an appearance and pretending to befriend, Cassio, as well as use Desdemona to bring about the downfall of two men, but he doesn't care! He relishes the prospect.

Shakespeare employs rhetorical questions to vividly show Iago's capability of turning good into evil. Is using a woman's *"goodness"* to bring about the ruin of Cassio and Othello the most contemptible of means? The images of poison and hell evoke the insidiousness of Iago's *"web"*, the animal imagery highlighting his bestial nature.

Section 4.6: Iago's Fifth Soliloquy

"I will in Cassio's lodging lose this napkin...
Which thou owedst yesterday."

This is a very short soliloquy, answering Emilia's previous musing as to what Iago will do with the *"handkerchief"*.

He will put it

"in Cassio's lodging...
And let him find it."

Iago reveals once again his knowledge of human nature. He remarks people who are jealous will see even the most trivial object as proof their jealousy is well-founded, as strong as *"Holy Writ"*.

Iago gloats,

"The Moor already changes with my poison",

having deduced jealousy is one of *"nature's poisons"*. Even if a person initially finds the feeling distasteful, jealousy is not easily eradicated. It infects the *"blood"* and burns

"like the mines of sulphur".

The disease and pain imagery here highlight Othello's suffering and Iago viciously states there is no medicine, no *"drowsy syrups"*, to give Othello *"sweet sleep"*. The Moor will never know a good night's rest again. It is even implied, via the metaphor of sleep, Othello is heading towards death.

The images of poison and hell highlight Iago's evil and Othello's pain, for which, Iago states, there is no cure.

Section 4.7: Othello's Soliloquy

"This Iago is extremely honest and good ...
I'll not believe it."

In this soliloquy the audience realise Othello's gullibility. He believes Iago to be *"of exceeding honesty"*, which evokes a great deal of pity. The audience are aware of Iago's deceit, but Othello is duped.

Ironically, Othello does recognise Iago is

"a learned spirit of human dealings",

but cannot see he has been studied and is being led like an *"ass"*.

To his credit Othello wishes to have proof of Desdemona's infidelity and thanks Fortune he is *"black"*, old and does not have to follow the social niceties of the Venetian *"chamberers"*; but he is hurting.

"She's gone. I am abused",

he laments and wishes he could *"loathe her"*. Only when he hates her may he find *"relief"*.

He views Desdemona as a possession and curses marriage because, although she is his wife, he has no control over her *"appetites"*, her desires or her whims. The thought of sharing her with others is repugnant. He'd rather be *"a toad"*, living in a *"dungeon"*, than a cuckold.

Othello, via disease imagery, puts forward the notion that *"great ones"* (important men) are more likely to be betrayed than poorer men. Is he right? Do *"great ones"* have more to loose and are they destined to suffer the *"plague"* of betrayal?

Finally he claims he will not believe Desdemona's infidelity, but are his words heartfelt?

In this soliloquy the audience is made aware of Othello's suffering and, despite some insight into Iago's personality, he cannot see how he is being duped. He is hurt by his wife's supposed betrayal and wonders: are *"great"* men destined to be betrayed?

Section Five: Techniques

Section 5. 1: Dramatic Devices

<u>1. Actions and stage directions</u>
Unlike many playwrights Shakespeare does not dwell on stage direction, nor does he write longwinded scene settings. For this reason his plays are open to interpretation by actors and directors; yet many directions are within the words of the play. For example Montano cries,

"I bleed still, I am hurt to the death",

following the brawl where Cassio is later demoted, proving Montano has been injured.

In the same scene Iago warns Montano,

"Touch me not so near",

revealing Montano may be pushing Iago literally to reveal the truth of his actions in the brawl.

Another example is where Lodovico demands in Act V,

"Wrench his sword from him",

instructing Iago be disarmed.

Shakespeare does, however, include the occasional direction by way of stating that the words are an *"aside"* or an instruction to *"stab"* or *"wound"*.

Actors are also shown when their characters actually die, enter the stage or leave.

<u>2. Describing events off stage</u>
Some events were too difficult to actually stage, therefore a character will reveal what is happening off-stage. In

Othello, the war against the Turks and the arrival of the victorious Moor is described by Montano and three gentlemen. Cassio's arrival with news that Othello may be lost at sea adds tension, but a messenger quickly re-establishes Othello's victory.

Do not forget Shakespeare was hindered by the limits of the stage and war was often depicted with the sounds of thunder, drums and the carrying of flags representing the warring parties.

3. Pronouncements
A herald comes to the fore in Act II to make a proclamation that Othello wishes for all his men to celebrate the victory over the Turks. Pronouncements allow for the plot to move forward quickly and to ensure that place and time are defined.

4. Letters
The reading of letters reveals the truth of what has passed. Roderigo leaves a letter, found at the end of the play, revealing Iago's machinations. It neatly summarises events: Roderigo has paid Iago to bring him favour with Desdemona and it was Iago who plotted to kill Cassio. Iago's guilt is thus confirmed by documentation.

Section 5.2: Music

Shakespeare used music in this play to denote several concepts: the arrival of a character, the celebration of war and to stress the theme of love. It is also an image used to show that men too can be played like instruments.

In Act II Scene I Othello arrives in Cyprus having been victorious in war. The trumpet sounds and Iago says,

> *"The Moor. I know his trumpet"*,

implying Othello has his own personal trumpeter to announce his arrival and the music played signals victory. A trumpet also heralds the arrival of Lodovico, Desdemona and attendants in Act IV Scene I, reflecting their higher status in society.

The soldiers sing songs in celebration of their victory over the Turk and Iago uses the opportunity to ply Cassio with wine during their songs. *"Some wine hoa"*, he repeatedly calls like a chorus and sings,

> *"Let a soldier drink"*.

These drinking songs encourage Cassio to drink more, satisfying Iago's plan to bring about the lieutenant's downfall.

The tolling of the bell following the fight between Cassio and Roderigo in Act II Scene II creates tension and stresses the *"death"* of Cassio's *"reputation"*.

Music also emphasises the theme of love, as it is the subject matter of many songs. Music surrounds Desdemona and her womanliness is highlighted by her ability to *"sing"* and to *"play music"*. These are fine accomplishments according to Othello, and befitting for a lady of noble stature. It also highlights Desdemona's *"sweet"* nature and innocence.

As she prepares for bed in Act V, Desdemona sings the song *"Willow"*. She was taught the song by her mother's maid, Barbary, who suffered a misfortune similar to that of the woman in the song who is betrayed by her lover. Barbary even died singing *"Willow"* and Emilia does too. Cleverly, Shakespeare points out life imitates Art and vice versa.

Ironically it is Emilia who betrays her husband, albeit by revealing the truth. The song's lyrics suggest both men and women are unfaithful to one another, highlighting Othello's belief in Desdemona's adultery. To Desdemona, the song reflects a resigned acceptance of her alienation from Othello's affections, and singing it leads her to question Emilia about the nature and practice of infidelity. Emilia later views the song as a warning.

> *"What did thy song bode Lady?"*

she asks Desdemona's corpse realising, as she too dies, the song boded ill for both of them and they should have heeded the song's lyrics.

When Othello fears his love for Desdemona has been tainted by her suspected adultery Shakespeare uses musical imagery to stress the love Othello felt for his wife. Othello laments the loss of love by referring to the departure of music from his life.

> *"Farewell the neighing steed, and the shrill trump,*
> *The spirit-stirring drum, th' ear piercing fife".*

The music of love is replaced by jealousy. Shakespeare employs music to be symbolic of happiness.

Iago repeatedly uses the image of men being played like instruments.

> *"Oh you are well tuned now, but I'll set down the pegs that make this music",*

he gloats on Othello's arrival in Cyprus. The audience is

reminded Iago is orchestrating a plan to bring about the Moor's ruin. In the final scene when Iago hears Cassio is still alive he comments.

"Then murder's out of tune",

suggesting his machinations have gone awry.

The image of men being played like instruments is akin to Shakespeare's popular image that men are mere puppets controlled on the world stage by the gods. Shakespeare is asking his audience to consider whether it is the gods who play mankind, or whether people are actually played or influenced by other men.

Music is integral to any production. It is used in film and theatre productions today to stress themes, create tension and mood. More banally, in Shakespeare's time, music hid the sounds of tramping feet across the stage and the movement of props and scenery. Yet Shakespeare was aware of the power of music. His songs rhymed and were easily remembered. The lyrics of many songs tell of love and the loss of love. They are often stories warning love can cause hurt, or are celebrations proving love can bring great happiness. Music is therefore not only associated with love but with victory and loss, accomplishment and influence.

Section 5.3: Literary Devices

Shakespeare was a poet as well as a playwright. He used all the literary devices available to him in his plays as well as in his poems, to the same effect: to create scenes, characters and images. Consider an example of each literary device in turn.

5.2.1: Repetition
Lines are repeated in *Othello* to emphasise how good and evil exist alongside each other. Iago repeats,

> *"I hate the Moor"*

yet he is repeatedly described as *"honest"*, reinforcing how he is fooling those around him.

"Sweet" is repeated as a term of endearment, but the words *"devil"* and *"monster"* are also reiterated, highlighting the good versus evil pervading the play.

5.2.2: Alliteration
This device is often used to stress a point. Emilia laments how Othello has insulted Desdemona,

> *"To be called whore, would it not make one weep?"*

The alliterative 'w' emphasises Desdemona is Othello's wife and aids the rhetorical questions uttered and the one unuttered: Why? Why does Othello call his wife a whore?

Iago uses alliteration to great effect when he plans to make Cassio drunk.

> *"Have I tonight fluster'd with flowing cups,*
> *And they watch too,*
> *Now amongst this flock of drunkards*
> *Am I to put our Cassio in some action*
> *That may offend the Isle."*

He has given all those on the watch plenty to drink and the alliterative 'f' highlights his foul intent and the foolishness of the men. The added metaphor that drunkards are a *"flock"* suggests the men will do Iago's bidding like sheep.

5.2.3: Rhyme
Remember rhyme is often used so people will recall lines, encouraging the contemplation of themes.

Rhyming couplets are used to denote the end of a scene and rhyme is also used to show reason, intellect and education. (Please read the next section for more insight).

5.2.4: Rhythm
The bulk of the play is written in blank verse. Lines from Iago's soliloquies are often remembered because of the rhythmical content and not because the rhyme. Listen to the eloquence of the soliloquies and the emotions evoked. Othello's pain is raw when he laments the murder of his wife.

> *"Whip me ye devils*
> *From the possession of this heavenly sight:*
> *Blow me about in winds of sulphur*
> *Wash me in steep-down gulfs of liquid fire."*

Iago's hatred of the Moor is viciously, yet rationally expressed in his soliloquies. His voice is measured, not profane, but reasoned, making this villain even more terrifying.

> *"I hate the Moor;*
> *And it is through abroad that 'twixt my sheets*
> *He's done my office."*

> *"The Moor, howbeit that I endure him not,*
> *Is of a constant loving, noble nature".*

Othello's quiet tone in his words at the end of the play, show the *"madness"* of *"jealousy"* has left him and he pleads,

> *" I pray you in your letters,*
> *When you shall these unlucky deeds relate,*
> *Speak of me as I am, nothing extenuate,*
> *Nor set down aught in malice."*

Rhythm thereby aids the voice of reason.

5.2.5: Rhetorical Questions

There are a number of rhetorical questions employed in the text to reinforce what is actually happening in the play and to echo what the audience may be thinking. Lodovico asks, when he sees Othello strike Desdemona,

> *"Are his wits safe? Is he not light of brain?"*

reminding the audience of Othello's recent *"epilepsy"* and reinforcing the question of whether he will *"strangle"* Desdemona.

The questions *"Why?"* and *"What?"* are frequently repeated, strengthening the tension and forcing the audience to ask, what will happen next and why Iago has put his machinations in motion?

5.2.6: Metaphor and Simile

The imagery in *Othello* is metaphoric, but I suggest particular attention is paid to Iago, who employs a wonderful turn of phrase. He tells Roderigo,

> *"I have professed to be thy friend, and I confess me knit to thy deserving with cables of perdurable toughness."*

Iago avows to tie himself to Roderigo's side and win *"fair Desdemona"*.

He tells the Moor in a moment of honesty,

> *"There's may a beast then in a populous city*
> *And many a civil monster."*

Poor Othello does not recognise the monster in his city is

Iago!

Desdemona too employs eloquent metaphors when she tells Cassio, she will speak to her husband on his behalf.

> *"His bed shall seem a school, his board a shrift;*
> *I'll intermingle everything he does with Cassio's suit".*

Desdemona intends to speak up for Cassio in the bedroom, the boardroom, everywhere and teach her misguided husband how he has misjudged his lieutenant.

Metaphors and similes are used as insults. Iago comments Othello is enraged and is *"like the Devil"* and of course Iago is called a number of epithets when his *"villainy"* comes to light in the final scene: *"demi-devil"; "Spartan dog"; "viper"* to name a few.

5.2.7: Contrast and Paradox

Repetition is used to convey the contrasting concepts of good and evil, but Shakespeare also employs two contrasting settings in his play to highlight emotion versus reason. (See later section for full analysis.) Venice is conveyed as a city of culture and reason, Cyprus, a place of emotional violence and turmoil.

The characters in the play contrast greatly. The black Moor, contrasts with the white Desdemona, highlighting the prejudice theme; *"honest"* Iago, contrasts with the truly honourable Cassio, both in turn at variance with Roderigo. Despite his evil nature, Iago is intelligent, Roderigo, a fool. Cassio shows integrity, whereas Roderigo does not. The appearance versus reality theme is brought to the fore.

Emilia, Bianca and Desdemona highlight the contrasting roles of women. Emilia, a woman of older years, worldly wise: Desdemona, the faithful wife and innocent victim; Bianca, a prostitute; but all are abused by their menfolk. The themes of love and punishment are to be pondered.

Paradox is most notable in Iago's views of *"reputation"*. He tells Cassio,

> *"Reputation is an idle and most false imposition, oft got without merit and lost without deserving."*

but later says to Othello,

> *"good name in man and woman, dear my lord is the immediate jewel of their soul."*

Shakespeare wishes his audience to consider which is true.

Section 5.4: Rhyme and Prose

Shakespeare wrote in blank verse, a rhythmical style that emulates speech. Prior to the Renaissance plays were performed in rhyme. This was somewhat unrealistic but it made the plays easier to remember by both performers and audience. Yet, rhyme can become monotonous, causing the audience's attention to wander.

It is employed in Shakespeare's plays to highlight erudition and intelligence. In the first act, the duke's answer to Brabantio's accusations against Othello are in blank verse.

"To vouch this is no proof,
Without more wider and more overt test
Than these thin habits and poor likelihoods
Of modern seeming do prefer against him."

Via rhyme the duke's status as a nobleman is assured. He is set above the other characters.

Iago's intelligence is highlighted too as he too uses blank verse, but Shakespeare cleverly adapts Iago's pattern of speech when he addresses Roderigo. Much of what Iago and Roderigo discuss is written in prose to reinforce the latter's foolish gullibility.

Cassio too speaks in prose when he is drunk, alcohol having tainted his intellect.

"Do not think gentlemen, I am drunk, this is my ancient, this is my right hand, and this is my left hand",

he says, in stark contrast to his pleas to Desdemona, hoping she will speak to Othello about his demotion.

"Madam, my former suit, I do beseech you
That, by your virtuous means, I may again
Exist and be a member of his love
Whom I with all the office of my heart

> *Entirely honour."*

Othello, in the throws of jealousy, speaks in prose. Having *"proof"* of Desdemona's adultery he tells Iago,

> *"Let her rot, and perish, and be damned tonight; for she shall not live. No, my heart is turned to stone. I strike it and it hurts my hand."*

Yet when he is of sound mind his words in blank verse are eloquent and heartfelt. Consider his defence in the wooing of Desdemona.

> *"Yet, by your patience,*
> *I will a round unvarnished tale deliver*
> *Of my whole course of love: what drugs what charms,*
> *What conjuration, and what mighty magic,*
> *For such proceedings I am charged withal -*
> *I won his daughter."*

In the final scene Othello is equally as eloquent.

> *"Set you down this;*
> *And say besides, that in Aleppo once*
> *Where a malignant and a turbaned Turk,*
> *Beat a Venetian and traduced the state,*
> *I took by th'throat the circumcised dog*
> *And smote him - thus."*

He then tragically and fatally stabs himself.

Rhyme is also a sign the scene has come to a close. Iago finishes the first act with the rhyming couplet,

> *"I have it, tis engender'd: hell and night*
> *Must bring this monstrous birth to the world's light."*

leaving the audience wondering if his evil plans will come to pass. The play too ends on a rhyming couplet, Lodovico stating,

> *"Myself will straight aboard, and to the state*
> *This heavy act with heavy heart relate."*

His final words reflect what the audience may do when leaving the theatre - relate the tale of the Moor of Venice to family and friends, urging them go see it.

Note that prose is used for more formal announcements: the Herald's proclamation and the sailor's report of the war for example.

However, be aware when Iago is lying his words are said in a more direct manner whereby the rhythmic quality is reduced. Consider when he tells Othello the outright falsehood of Cassio's words whilst sleeping.

> *"In sleep I heard him say, 'Sweet Desdemona'*
> *Let us be wary, let us hide our loves';*
> *And then sir, would he gripe and wring my hand,*
> *Cry, 'O sweet creature!' and then kiss me hard,*
> *As if he plucked up kisses by the roots ..."*

He then pours more *"pestilence"* into the ear of the unsuspecting Moor.

> *"Nay, but be wise: yet we see nothing done;*
> *She may be honest yet. Tell me but this:*
> *Have you not sometimes seen a handkerchief*
> *Spotted with strawberries in your wife's hand?"*

These words are not as lyrical as his soliloquies.

Rhyme and prose are therefore devices used by Shakespeare to highlight the themes of emotion versus reason, as prose is used when rationale is lost. Iago adapts his speech patterns when he is lying and when speaking with the gullible Roderigo. Finally, rhyming couplets conclude scenes and acts leaving the audience often wanting more.

Section 5.5: Irony

Shakespeare loved irony as it creates tension, adds erudition and interest to his plays. There are three kinds of irony utilised in *Othello*: verbal, situational and dramatic. All assist in the themes of appearance versus reality, love, deceit and betrayal, but it also heightens the suspense and creates a palpable tension.

<u>Verbal irony</u> is when characters say the opposite of what they mean, thus becoming an integral aspect of the appearance versus reality theme.

Iago is ensconced in verbal irony because he lies and, unfortunately, is believed.

> *"You know I love you,"*

he tells the Moor, but he has stated the exact opposite.

> *"I hate the Moor",*

he spits in his first soliloquy, relishing the opportunity to have his revenge.

He tells Cassio,

> *"You know I am an honest man,"*

but he is putting on a show. Yet at times he is brutally honest.

> *"I am not what I am".*

he states and claims to *"love"* Desdemona, not in a romantic sense but, ironically, because she will be the tool by which he will wreak his revenge on Cassio and Othello.

> *"Now I do love her too,*
> *Not out of absolute lust...*

> *...But partly led to diet my revenge."*

He also warns Othello famously,

> *"O, beware, my lord, of jealousy. It is the green-ey'd monster, which doth mock the meat it feeds on".*

Iago is twisted enough to tell the Moor not to let jealousy overcome his reason, but is Iago using reverse psychology? By mentioning jealousy, does he incite Othello to feel jealous?

Perhaps one of the best examples of verbal irony is when Iago speaks of *"reputation"*, beautifully twisting his words to appeal to his dupe. To Cassio he says,

> *"Reputation is an idle and most false imposition. Oft got without merit and lost without deserving."*

To Othello he states the exact opposite.

> *"Good name in man and woman, dear my lord is the immediate jewel of their soul."*

Via verbal irony Iago can endear himself to others, the audience left to wonder what the *"demi-devil"* truly believes.

<u>Situational irony</u> is when actions have the opposite effect to what was intended. In *Othello*, Iago machinates to bring about the demise of Cassio. Watching Cassio with Desdemona he gloats,

> *"With as little web as this I will ensnare as great a fly as Cassio."*

Ironically he fails but, tragically, he does bring about the death of Desdemona and, his wife, Emilia. Furthermore, Shakespeare employs a wonderful ironic twist when Cassio is left to decide Iago's fate.

Another example of situational irony concerns Othello's love for Desdemona. He states he will die rather than think his wife disloyal,

"My life upon her faith,"

he tells Brabantio, when the old man warns the Moor,

"She has deceived her father; and may thee".

At the end of the play, ironically, Othello does die because he suspects his wife of adultery.

Othello is also mistaken when he tells Iago,

*"Not from my own weak merits will I draw
The smallest fear or doubt of her revolt",*

believing his wife will remain true and he will not succumb to jealousy. He does, to such an extent he falls *"into an epilepsy"*, a *"savage madness"*.

<u>Dramatic irony</u> is when the audience is aware of something the characters are not.

Again this very much surrounds Iago as the audience is cognisant of his desire for revenge and Roderigo's *"fortune"*. Othello, Cassio and Roderigo are

"led by the nose like asses are."

The audience knows Iago is abusing Roderigo for *"sport and profit"* and he wishes to take Othello, *"wife for wife"*, believing the Moor has slept with Emilia. Furthermore the audience knows Iago plans to put Othello

*"into a jealousy so strong
That judgement cannot cure,"*

thus highlighting Iago's evil.

Dramatic irony heightens the tension in the play. The audience is rapt, wondering if Iago's vicious plans will come to pass or come to light. Arguably, because the audience is aware of Iago's intent, a greater pity for Desdemona and Othello is also emoted.

Irony is a tool expertly wielded by Shakespeare to make his play more entertaining, more suspenseful and certainly more interesting. Notice how from goodness, evil can spring and how deep-rooted emotions can conquer reason. Irony highlights the evils and weaknesses of humankind, but even more ironically, four hundred years have passed since Shakespeare wrote this play and mankind still hasn't learned!

Section 5.6: Settings

The map of the world was remarkably different in Shakespeare's time than it is today. Italy was not one unified country, it was an area made up of states, provinces and realms, ruled by different leaders. The Pope held sway in Rome, Florence was a republic, Naples a kingdom, but Venice was ruled by a senate, headed by a duke, or doge. It was a cosmopolitan city due to the new trade routes opening up to the east and it was fiercely independent from the religious influence of Rome. Venetians prided themselves on their sophistication, political modernity and culture.

Italy to Shakespeare's audience would have been a reminder of the artists such as Leonardo da Vinci or Michelangelo, wonderful creators of fine Art, but it had a darker side too. Niccolo Machiavelli, had written a work entitled *The Prince*, in which he cast aside the concept of leaders being virtuous and God's representative on Earth. Instead, he proclaimed all that mattered in politics was the achievement of power and control. Can you see a reflection of this concept in the actions of the *"demi-devil"*, Iago?

Venice, to Shakespeare's audience, was a place of art, culture and worldliness. It was considered the centre of the world due to its location in the Mediterranean, half way to the east. It welcomed travellers and tradesmen, thus foreigners were a daily occurrence in the city. London too was a busy port, welcoming discoveries from the New World of America and Shakespeare knew his audience would see comparisons between the two cities.

Cyprus was viewed as entirely different to Venice. Simply put, the island was a stronghold in the Mediterranean Sea, where rule fluctuated between the Ottoman Empire, (now Turkey) and Europe. It was the scene of many battles, thus becoming, in *Othello*, a metaphor for turmoil.

Recall how Othello loses his mind on the island, and Cassio loses his reason, resorting to brawling when Iago plies him with alcohol. Even Iago's machinations and desire for revenge can be seen to be the product of tumultuous emotions. Where peace, tolerance and sophistication were associated with Venice, Cyprus reflected violence, upheaval and potential war. In short, Venice was a place of reason, Cyprus, the locale for emotion; thereby the settings become very much entwined with the theme of emotion versus reason.

Finally, another setting alluded to is the birthplace of *"the Moor"*: North Africa, directly opposite Italy and the southern coast of Europe. The Barbary Coast was renowned for its pirates and slave trade, therefore many viewed those from North Africa as potentially dangerous. Othello, an eloquent soldier is in stark contrast to the stereotypical expectation of a North African Moor. The theme of appearance versus reality is highlighted here.

The irony of the play is the cultured, but Machiavellian, Venetian, Iago, viciously orchestrates the downfall of the North African, Othello, whereas Shakespeare's audience would have expected the 'barbarous' Moor, to bring about the ruin of the prosperous Italians.

Shakespeare chose his settings carefully ensuring the audience would equate them with the two main themes of emotion versus reason and appearance versus reality. Although the action takes place several hundred miles away from England, a more erudite theatregoer would recognise the similarities between Venice and London, posing the question: who among the crowds, in the Court, in the army, in the marketplace, was the English equivalent to Iago?

Section Six: Essay Plans

Section 6.1: Introduction to Essay Plans

The plans that follow contain some quotes and many rhetorical questions Shakespeare hopes the audience considers. Refer to the previous notes when answering questions, wherein lie other quotes and references.

Extra quotes will be needed to make the essays more scholarly and it is often a good idea to offer an opinion and reference a production. It is best to refer to professional productions easily recognised by an examiner. I tend to cite Orson Welles' version, and Oliver Parker's brilliant production (as this is a personal favourite), starring Laurence Fishburne and Kenneth Branagh, although there are many others worthy of mention,

Furthermore, to show the examiner the play has merit in today's world, a modern reference may be included but do not become side-tracked. Keep to the question asked and include the keyword(s) of the question in the answer.

DO NOT TELL THE STORY UNLESS SPECIFICALLY ASKED. Many candidates come unstuck by simply telling the examiner who did what when. The trick to writing on *Othello* is to reference the themes, characters or images including quotes, an opinion and citing a production. It is the latter which make essays unique and interesting.

The plans that follow are only GUIDELINES to answers. They are not THE ANSWERS! Take time in writing essays and be sure not to repeat points.

Good luck and happy studying

A E Chambers

Section 6.2: Plan for an essay on Fear and Pity in *Othello*

<u>Introduction</u>: Fear and pity are the two elements of Shakespearean tragedy. What Shakespeare's audience, in the seventeenth century, feared is both similar yet different to what many fear today. The play has to be read in context, considering contemporary and modern audiences.

The question as to whether the audience pities the characters is subjective and open to change depending on the production seen and the mood of the individual.

Fear

<u>Point 1:</u> Fear of evil: Iago is a terrifying character in that he is able to manipulate people to his will and orchestrate events to serve his own purpose. More terrifying perhaps is that his purpose is understandable: thwarted ambition and revenge.

His insidious behaviour is a warning of not to judge others by their appearance. Iago is seen as *"honest"* and he presents himself as a soldier. More frighteningly he has a tendency to tell the truth, but for his own underhand gain. He has a way with words, telling Cassio *"reputation"* is unimportant, then telling Othello a man's *"reputation"* is precious.

Iago can be viewed as a very evil and fearsome character because he has the ability to control his emotions. He, of all the characters, can keep a cool head. His final words,

"From this time forth I never will speak word"

shows he can control his feelings. His statement

"I hate the Moor"

is said in soliloquy and none of the characters suspect Iago's intense dislike for Othello, such is his ability to hide his inner thoughts.

Point 2: Fear of death: The fear of being sent to hell if one does not die in a State of Grace was severe amongst the seventeenth century populace. Although the concept of God was under review in the Renaissance, many believed in the punishment of hell and the reward of heaven. Othello is concerned for Desdemona

"Have you prayed tonight?"

he asks her, opening the question as to whether he wishes her further punishment in hell, or to be sent to heaven.

Point 3: Fear of losing one's reputation: Othello is concerned in his final speech that he be remembered for having done

"the state some service".

He's beaten the Turkish fleet (the *"circumcised dog"*) and saved Venice from attack. He realises he could be remembered only for his final acts of uxoricide and suicide, which would taint his reputation as a *"commander"*. He fears his final deeds will outweigh his victories.

After Cassio has been demoted he laments repeatedly,

"My reputation ... my reputation".

He fears that he has lost the *"immortal part"* of himself and become *"bestial"*, as low as an animal. Cassio believes a man's *"name"* will afford him success and he fears to lose it will bring hardship and ignominy.

Point 4: Fear of madness: Othello's intense jealousy sends him *"mad"*, which was fearful to Shakespeare's audience as madness implied an asylum where the inmates faced a slow demise.

For a man of reason to succumb to madness is even more frightening. Othello has a high rank, a high intelligence and all his learning and ability and wealth do not prevent him from falling *"into an epilepsy"*.

Point 5: Fear of war: The beginning of the play is set against a backdrop of war when the Venetians are facing attack from the Turk. War brought both riches if won, but hardship if lost. The uncertainty of war caused great fear among the populace. Regardless of the eventual outcome however, war often resulted in poverty leading to famine, plague and the demise of a population, especially of the stronger younger men on whom many were reliant.

Point 6: Fear of thunder and lightning: Today the weather is understood, but in Shakespeare's day thunder and lightning were viewed as a warning from the gods (God), or a portent for troubled times. The storm whilst the war is waging highlights the fear of war and the tempestuous suffering of Othello as his jealousy descends into madness.

The inclusion of thunder and lightning is, of course, dependent on the director, but a *"desperate tempest"* is discussed when the sea battle is described at the beginning of the second act.

Pity
The amount of sympathy an audience would have with the characters is subjective and dependent on the production,

Othello: Is a victim of racial prejudice. Desdemona's father is appalled his daughter has married a man of *"sooty"* complexion. Brabantio accuses Othello of using *"witchcraft"* to ensnare his daughter, but Othello explains that it was simply his *"good manners"* and his life story that caused Desdemona to *"pity"* him and subsequently fall in love with him.

The Duke of Venice praises the Moor and knows Othello is the *"best"* man to command his fleet against the Turk. Thus

Othello is regarded highly by his fellow soldiers, except, of course, by Iago who is enraged by the Moor.

How much sympathy is extended to Othello because of his ethnicity? Can the audience pity Othello, as he is a victim of Iago's machinations?

Can Othello be pitied because he is the victim of a truly competent and capable, insidious villain? Remember, Othello has no reason to doubt Iago's venomous words regarding Desdemona's infidelity, as Iago orchestrates the *"proof"* he requires.

However, Othello does not face Cassio, neither does he reason with his wife. His jealousy takes hold and he loses his ability to rationalise Desdemona's regard for Cassio as a loyal soldier and not as a lover. Is his act of uxoricide reason not to pity him?

Roderigo: is also a victim of Iago's machinations, but he is far more gullible than Othello, yet equally blinded by his love for Desdemona. Iago encourages Roderigo repeatedly to

"put money in thy purse",

meaning he will have to have the financial means to impress the lady, but also that he should act to ensure his love is made known. Can the audience pity a man who is enamoured with another man's wife? Is Roderigo's foolishness a reason not to pity him? Can Roderigo be pitied as he is masterfully duped by Iago, losing his life and his *"fortune"*?

Cassio: is a victim of Iago's insidious plot too. Yet, Cassio has freewill to decide on his actions, albeit manipulated by Iago. It is Cassio's decision to take more than *"one cup"* of wine following the victory against the Turk. Cassio admits he has

"very poor and unhappy brains for drinking"

yet he takes the brew Iago proffers. Cassio falls neatly into Iago's trap to fight with Roderigo, which leads to his demotion and loss of *"reputation"*. Can the audience feel any pity for a man who over indulges in alcohol?

Can pity be extended to Cassio when Desdemona's handkerchief is found in his room, which he then gives to Bianca? He is the innocent victim of Iago's plotting. Furthermore he is the innocent in a conversation he has with Iago about his dalliance with Bianca. Iago orchestrates the conversation to be overheard by Othello, who believes the two men are discussing Desdemona. This is a brilliant orchestration that leads Othello to declare:

"How shall I murder him, Iago?"

putting Cassio's life in danger.

What is questionable about Cassio is his inability to plead his case to Othello directly. His action to ask Desdemona to put in a good word for him and restore his good name is not the act of a courageous warrior. Can an audience feel pity for such an ineffective soldier? Or, once again, can Iago's mastery be a mitigating circumstance?

<u>Desdemona</u>: is probably the character an audience would pity the most. She is not only a victim of Iago's *"diet"* of revenge, but also a victim of Othello's jealousy.

She truly loves Othello, defying her filial duty to marry the Moor. She innocently entertains Cassio's entreaties for her to speak to her husband, following his demotion, and she weeps when she discovers the handkerchief, Othello's *"first gift"*, has gone missing.

Othello's decision to kill his wife ensures the audience will pity this Venetian woman. She is completely innocent of all charges claimed by her husband and she dies, unabsolved of her alleged sins.

Emilia and Bianca: are depicted as *"food"* to satisfy the lusts of men. Emilia is a victim of uxoricide and Bianca is abused by Cassio. He refers to her as a *"customer"* implying prostitute and will never marry her. Shakespeare has been seen as one of the first feminist writers, viewing women in a more realistic light. Although his audience may not have had any sympathy for women, who were viewed as chattels and whores, more modern audiences can feel some pity for these women.

Iago: Can anyone have pity for, arguably, Shakespeare's most villainous villain? The fact he has been overlooked for promotion may instil feelings of understanding for his resentment, but is this negated because of his selfish, insidious and murderous actions? Can he be pitied for the likelihood of being tortured?

Conclusion: People still fear death, infirmity of mind, and continue to be unaware of the more fearful characters infesting a society, continuing to judge by appearance. Some still fear thunder and lightning, war and the loss of reputation. How much pity can be bestowed on the characters is subjective, and reliant of performance, but Shakespeare's work still inspires discussion and provokes thought.

Section 6.3: Plan for an essay on Drama and Intrigue in *Othello*

<u>Introduction</u>: *Othello,* being a tragedy, has to have the expected elements of Shakespearean tragedy: fear and pity. All good drama also requires tension or suspense, brought about by intrigue, with the added bonuses of sex and violence.

<u>Point 1</u>: Tension is heightened by the intrigue woven in the play. Via Iago's asides and soliloquies the audience is aware of Iago's intent, whereas the characters are not. (Dramatic irony.)

The audience are caught up in Iago's *"web"*, encouraging numerous questions: Will his plans unfold? Who will live and who will die? Will he be caught? What will his punishment be?

<u>Point 2</u>: The violence of the play aids the drama. Consider the brawl prior to Cassio's demotion, the wounding of Montano, the murders of Roderigo, Desdemona and Emilia, not forgetting the wounding of Cassio and Othello's suicide.

Even off stage the violent backdrop of the war against the Turk heightens the turmoil within Cyprus.

<u>Point 3</u>: Sex is mentioned on many occasions in *Othello*, but the actual deed is not seen on stage (maybe in more modern film versions). Consider Othello and Desdemona's (blind) love, Cassio's relationship with Bianca and Iago seeing women as *"sport"*. Furthermore Emilia puts forward the image of women as food to sate men's appetites.

<u>Point 4</u>: Fear is highlighted via deceit. Desdemona deceives her father, Iago deceives everyone. Fear is also manifested in Othello's madness and the punishments endured by the characters, highlighted by hell, monster and pain imagery.

Point 5: Pity may be extended to Desdemona the innocent victim, but how much can the audience pity the other characters? (Refer to previous essay plan.)

Cassio is coerced to become drunk by Iago and severely punished by Othello. Can Othello be pitied as he is fooled by a master manipulator?

Conclusion: The tension mounts due to the intrigue. Drama is created by instilling fear into the hearts of the audience, encouraging them to pity the characters and via the violence and contrasting love stories.

Section 6.4: Plan for an essay on The Minor Characters in *Othello*

<u>Introduction</u>: Shakespeare's minor characters are relevant to themes in the play and highlight the flaws and attributes of the major characters, Iago, Othello and Desdemona.

<u>Brabantio</u>: highlights Desdemona's choice between filial duty and spousal duty. He also brings to the fore the prejudice theme in the play, condemning Othello due to his colour, expecting his daughter to marry a man of equal status.

<u>Lodovico</u>: emphasises the emotion versus reason theme in the play. He is the voice of Venetian reason in contrast to Othello's obsessive jealousy and violence towards Cassio and Desdemona. He is shocked by Othello's barbaric behaviour.

<u>Roderigo</u>: contrasts with Iago being jealous of Othello. Where Iago is jealous of Othello's rank and suspicious of his lechery; Roderigo envies Othello's marriage to Desdemona.

Roderigo's love for Desdemona is akin to Othello in that he sees her as pure and *"sweet"*, but thinks he can buy her love, whereas Othello has earned it.

His gullibility is similar to Othello's in that he is fooled and betrayed by Iago. He too is persuaded by flattery and deceived by Iago using his flaw: not being able to see the truth behind Iago's mask.

<u>Cassio</u>: is a foil for Iago (a contrasting opposite), stressing the appearance versus reality theme. *"Honest"* Iago is revealed as the insidious villain, Cassio, appearing the honourable nobleman and he proves his worth by not being jealous, nor vengeful.

He treasures his reputation, but like the other characters he is deceived by Iago via his flaw of being a poor drinker.

This flaw is not as profound as Othello's jealousy (as drinking and sexual lusts were tolerated in a nobleman's society). Neither is it as profound as Roderigo's foolishness or Brabantio's prejudice.

Bianca: highlights the love / lust theme, where women sate men's sexual appetites. Consider how Cassio exploits her.

Emilia: is torn between spousal duty and a duty to her mistress, Desdemona, over the handkerchief. Emilia later reasons her husband insidious villain. As a woman and servant she is expected to be "*simple*" but, highlighting the appearance versus reality theme, she proves to be intelligent and betrays her husband as she dies.

Note: Emilia, Cassio and Roderigo are all abused by Iago. Without these three characters, would Iago be as insidious or as villainous? Surely not as his schemes would only affect Othello and Desdemona.

Conclusion: Brabantio highlights prejudice and duty. Lodovico is the voice of reason amongst turbulent emotions. Cassio is the foil to Iago, highlighting noble traits versus insidious ones. Consider here too the appearance versus the reality theme. Roderigo compares with Othello, both fooled by Iago. Bianca highlights the theme of lust and love and Emilia the themes of duty, appearance versus reality and betrayal. Without the minor characters Iago's schemes may make him a lesser villain.

Section 6.5: Plan for an essay on
"It is the evil that enthrals the audience in the play, *Othello*, not the good." Discuss this statement with reference to and quotation from the play.

Introduction: *Othello* is a play where good and evil reside side by side. Via the appearance versus reality theme, it is often difficult to distinguish which character is good, which evil. Which is more enthralling is up to the individual to decide.

Yes, evil enthrals the audience

Point 1: Iago is a compelling, manipulator of Othello, Roderigo and Cassio. He even urges Emilia to steal the handkerchief. He incites Othello's jealousy, plays on Roderigo's love for Desdemona and orchestrates a brawl to bring about Cassio's demotion, later encouraging him to ask Desdemona to speak for him.

Iago's villainy is certainly enthralling. There is a perversity in loving to hate Iago.

Point 2: Fear created in the play may enthral the audience. Consider how easily Othello becomes mad with jealousy, how emotions overcome reason.

Point 3: The violence in the play is enthralling, with the murders of Roderigo, Emilia and Desdemona. Othello's suicide is also violent.

Point 4: Brabantio's racism and the male character's sexism are social evils that may enthral the audience.

No, goodness enthrals the audience

Point 1: The love stories within the play are enthralling. Consider Othello's tale of how he wooed Desdemona and her wish to accompany her husband to Cyprus.

She is pure and innocent, choosing to do her spousal duty rather than her filial duty.

Desdemona is punished for a sin she did not commit and elicits a great deal of pity. Is this not enthralling?

Point 2: Cassio shows goodness when he values his reputation and shows a regard and respect for Desdemona. Iago abuses this sorely and the audience can pity him. Can this enthral an audience?

Point 3: Emilia emotes goodness towards her mistress and friend, Desdemona. She is torn between a love for her friend and her spousal duty. She pays a high price for her intelligence and loyalty. Is their relationship enthralling?

Point 4: Goodness triumphs in the denouement of the play, when Emilia reasons her husband's treachery and Roderigo's letters reveal Iago's machinations. The idea of good winning out over evil, is this enthralling?

Conclusion: Whether evil enthrals the audience more than goodness is left to the individual to decide. The play relies on good and evil existing side by side, one highlighting the other. Iago's manipulations certainly enthral, but so do the love stories. The violence is tempered by friendship and the fear by pity. Although, goodness triumphs, it does at a terrible cost, the tragedy has the power to enthral and captivate audiences for hundreds of years.

Section 6.6: Plan for an essay on

"Othello's foolishness rather than Iago's cleverness leads to the tragedy of Shakespeare's *Othello*." Discuss this statement supporting your answer with the aid of suitable reference to the text.

<u>Introduction:</u> Iago's knowledge and ability to manipulate brings about the downfall of a naive, jealous Othello, whose overwhelming love for his wife leads to tragedy.

<u>Point 1</u>: Iago is calculating not allowing his hatred of the Moor to overcome his vengeance. He uses his head to bring about the downfall of Othello. Refer to the plans he makes in his soliloquies.

<u>Point 2</u>: Iago is clever knowing the Moor loves Desdemona deeply and his hamartia, his jealousy, will lead to his ruin but, Iago has no true idea as to what Othello will actually do. It is therefore because he

"loved wisely, not too well",

Othello is undone, not through his foolishness, but by loving Desdemona.

<u>Point 3</u>: Othello is too trusting as he believes his ancient to be *"honest"*. Is this foolish or naive? It certainly shows poor judgement. Iago is clever enough to use his high standing to dupe the Moor.

<u>Point 4</u>: Othello is wise demanding Iago show *"proof"* of Desdemona's infidelity, yet, Iago is clever enough to provide such proof. Othello sees Cassio with his handkerchief and overhears him speak of a supposed liaison with Desdemona. Unfortunately he believes the conversation is about his wife, when it is about Bianca, but what evidence is there for him to doubt it? None!

<u>Point 5</u>: Othello may be foolish believing Iago's tales of Cassio's treachery with his wife, but Iago is quick-witted

when he reiterates Brabantio's warning of the possibility of Desdemona's betrayal. Iago is a master manipulator, an opportunist and a good judge of character; Othello, is not. Is Othello's *"honest"* nature his undoing? Can this be construed as foolishness?

Point 6: The tragedy of the play is Othello does not confront Desdemona with his suspicions until he is firmly convinced she has cuckolded him. Is this an act of foolishness or an act of a man driven to madness? Iago's *"poison"* has worked as he has taken every opportunity to pour thoughts of Desdemona's betrayal into Othello's ear. Is this cleverness or opportunism? Was it foolish of Othello to believe him, or did Iago give him all the *"proof"* he needed?

Conclusion: Iago is intelligent and does not allow the emotion of hate to cloud his vengeance. Iago is clever enough to manipulate Othello's feelings and put on a pretence to disguise his hatred of the man. He is smart enough to know his commander's flaws and use them against him. He is quick-witted and persistent, pouring *"pestilence"* into Othello's ear, contriving *"proof"* of Desdemona's infidelity.

However, none of this would have had the resultant effect if Othello had not been foolish enough to believe his ancient to be *"honest"* and for not facing Desdemona earlier with his doubts. It is because Othello loves his wife and because he is *"honest"*, Iago is able to bring about the man's ruin, not because Othello is altogether foolish.

Section 6.7: Plan for an essay on "Desdemona is just too good to be true." Discuss with quotation from and reference to the play *Othello*.

Introduction: Desdemona is often viewed as the epitome of Jacobean womanhood. She is demure, loving and dutiful, but is torn between filial duty to her father and spousal duty to her husband. She is the innocent victim of uxoricide and is often seen as being goodness personified. Yet Desdemona has a wilful streak and is, like all characters in *Othello*, flawed, thus can be seen as being too good to be true.

Point 1: Desdemona exhibits an independence that confounds Brabantio and her husband. She defies her father by marrying Othello without his consent. She speaks up asking the duke to allow her to go to Cyprus with her husband, and demands Othello speak to her about Cassio's demotion, which enrages him. She is not the epitome of Jacobean womanhood, subservient to her menfolk, but a woman in her own right.

Point 2: She is oblivious to Othello's jealous nature as she is blinded by her love for him. She views him as an adventurer, brave and strong and not as a jealous *"green ey'd monster"*. Her lack of prejudice shows she is indeed good, but her hamartia is she loves too much.

Point 3: Her blindness extends to other characters. She cannot see Iago's machinations believing, like her husband, Iago is *"honest"*, nor Emilia's betrayal with the handkerchief. She is somewhat naive.

Point 4: Desdemona is capable of reason, rationalising her duty is to her husband and not her father, emulating her mother, but she allows her emotions to cloud her reason and is once again blinded. She reckons pursuing Cassio's suit with Othello is an act of friendship and loyalty. Can this be seen as honourable? She does not foresee Othello's jealous anger. She becomes distraught when she looses the handkerchief, not thinking she is a victim of theft.

Point 5: Even on her deathbed she cannot foresee Othello's murderous intentions and Emilia and Iago's deception. Her capability of trusting too much proves to be a flaw.

Point 6:   Love of her husband ironically causes Desdemona's ruin. She is an innocent victim, falsely accused of adultery and wrongly executed.

Conclusion: Desdemona is a fine woman who is too good to be true. She has an independent spirit that enrages her father and her husband. She is blinded by love, which overcomes her powers of reason and as a dutiful wife is betrayed by her husband, her friend, Emilia and is sorely abused by Iago.

Section 6.8: Plan for an essay on
Why Study *Othello* in the 21st Century?

<u>Introduction</u>: The play is over 400 years old, but the emotions, characters and themes still resonate; thus it has great relevance in today's world.

<u>Point 1</u>: Othello's jealousy results in the demise of his wife. Consider divorce statistics through infidelity.

<u>Point 2</u>: Roderigo's jealous of Othello's marriage to Desdemona. The American soap opera, *Dallas,* was recently resurrected and one of the most famous cliff-hangers was the question: who shot JR? It transpired it was JR's sister in law, jealous of her sister's marriage to JR!

<u>Point 3</u>: Iago is jealous of Cassio's position. How far will some go in the corporate world to ensure aggrandisement?

<u>Point 4</u>: Jealousy was as destructive in Shakespeare's time as it is now. Consider how Shakespeare's metaphor of it being the *"green ey'd monster"* has endured.

<u>Point 5</u>: Even today people allow their emotions to cloud their reason. Othello loses his reason and becomes mad. Who has lost their reason, job and reputation recently?

<u>Point 6</u>: Cassio loses his reason via alcohol. Anyone spring to mind who has lost their livelihood or reputation due to drunken behaviour.

<u>Point 7</u>: Punishment is as relevant today as it was years ago. What should Iago's punishment be? Did Desdemona deserve to be punished? Consider the use of torture and the innocent being collateral damage in today's world.

<u>Point 8</u>: Is Othello's suicide justified? Seen as noble by Othello, but also viewed as 'easy way out', a cowardly way out. Several well known celebrities have taken their own lives. Anyone compare with Othello?

Point 9: Deceit, deception and appearance versus reality still abound. Othello appears a valiant warrior, but in reality a tortured soul. Soldiers returning from war zones, despite their uniforms many are suffering from PTSD.

Iago appears *"honest"* but so do conmen. Iago takes Rodrigo's money under false pretences. Has this occurred lately?

Point 10: Love being blind. Othello and Desdemona's love blind each other to their faults. Anyone in the news come to mind?

Emilia betrays her husband. Today wives can testify against their husbands but they don't have to.

Point 11: Prejudice still exists in world. Racial prejudice and sexism are very relevant in today's world. Compare the treatment of Bianca and Emilia to recent examples.

Point 12: Shakespeare's plays have longevity because they have all the attributes of fine drama: violence, sex, tension, suspense and irony. Consider some television shows and films employing all these techniques.

Conclusion: Times change, people don't. The study of *Othello* is a lesson not to allow emotions to cloud reason, not to be taken in by appearance, to love moderately and beware of prejudice. Directors, producers and writers still look to Shakespeare for ideas and techniques bringing quality drama into the homes of billions every day, to instruct and entertain. The play is well worthy of study as a warning to all.

NOTE: This essay has to contain more on *Othello* than on 21st century. Reference ONE example of the here and now ensuring to keep the essay on point to Shakespeare's play.

Section 6.9: Plan for an essay on Why Do the Characters Trust Each Other?

<u>Introduction</u>: People trust others for three reasons, all of which are apparent in *Othello*. People trust others when their previous behaviour has proven them trustworthy, people trust others when they are blinded by their emotions and people trust others judging them by their appearance.

<u>People trust others on what they have done in the past.</u>

<u>Point 1:</u> The characters have no reason not to trust each other. Othello trusts Iago as it is implied he has been loyal, (until now!) Iago has been *"honest"* and only the promotion of Cassio and the belief that Othello has dallied with Emilia causes his desire for revenge.

<u>Point 2:</u> The senators have no reason not to trust Othello as he has been an exemplary commander. Lodovico trusts Othello on his past victories and has seen him as a reasoned man.

<u>Point 3</u>: Brabantio, Othello and Cassio all trust Desdemona due to her previous demure behaviour. When Othello tells of his wooing of Desdemona she appears as a stereotypical Jacobean woman. Cassio refers to her as beautiful and worthy.

<u>People trust others because they are blinded by emotion.</u>

<u>Point 4:</u> Roderigo trusts Iago as he is blinded by his love for Desdemona and his desire to woo her. Emotion makes Roderigo gullible and Iago exploits this.

<u>Point 5:</u> Desdemona is blinded by her love for Othello and cannot see nor understand his jealousy. She even trusts him on her deathbed. She is also blinded by his initial appearance and tales of daring-do.

Point 6: Emilia chooses to blind herself to the possible machinations of her husband when she gives him the handkerchief. It is unknown as to whether she has any real inkling as to what Iago will do with it.

People judge others by their appearance.

Point 7: An audience judges characters as noble or honourable due to their appearance and rank. People tend to trust others of a similar or higher rank to themselves. Emilia trusts Othello and Desdemona due to their higher rank. The audience and Emilia are shocked when Othello proves to be flawed. Brabantio does not trust Othello as he sees him as being inferior to himself.

Iago is trusted because of his demeanour, eloquence and military rank. He lies, but his words ring true. His actions are self-serving, but he puts on an act of friendship others do not doubt.

Conclusion: Shakespeare warns his audience not be so trusting. People are fickle. People lie. People put on a show. Do not trust by appearance, beware as people hide their true feelings and are blinded by their emotions. Finally be aware people change and just because they have proved worthy in the past does not mean they are to be trusted in the future.

Section 6.10: Plan for an essay on
The Treatment of Women in *Othello*.

Introduction: Women in the seventeenth century did not have the privileges they have today. They were very much viewed as second-class citizens and had few choices in life. In *Othello*, Shakespeare brings to he fore how men saw women as possessions and *"food"* to satiate their sexual *"appetites"*, a *"sport"* in the bedchamber. However, he subtly portrays Desdemona as a beautiful, independent, spirited woman, Emilia an intuitive wife, torn between spousal duty and friendship and Bianca, a naive courtesan or prostitute, abused by Cassio and Iago.

Point 1: Brabantio is very protective of his daughter, Desdemona. He deems Roderigo as unworthy, telling him plainly,

"My daughter is not for thee",

and is enraged when he hears she has defied him by marrying Othello without asking his permission. It is as if she is his to give away.

"How got she out?"

he asks as if he keeps her like a pet. He is a reminder of how women were used as tools to create alliances, fortify powerbases and increase wealth.

Point 2: Desdemona is praised for her beauty and sweet nature by Othello and Cassio. Looks and the ability to bear children appear to be important to the men in the play and there is the expectation women will be subservient and demure. Shakespeare had a more realistic opinion of women, knowing that beneath their beauty and childbearing capabilities they were individuals in their own right.

Point 3: Othello is accused of bewitching Desdemona with *"spells"* and *"charms"*, although on closer study, she seems to have more influence over him, than he over her. Iago says,

"Our general's wife is now the general",

and the Moor is so in love with her, he cannot deny her anything. Shakespeare noted women could exert a fascination over their menfolk.

Consider how Roderigo is so enamoured with Desdemona, he is prepared to die rather than live without her.

Point 4: Shakespeare uses Desdemona to highlight how women were torn by filial duty to their parents, (Commandment Number Five) and the marriage vow. Desdemona tells her father she will emulate her mother, but for other women it was not so straightforward. She is forthright in her decision and at the end of the play the audience learns Brabantio has died of a broken heart, unable to reconcile his daughter's decision with his own opinion.

Point 5: Desdemona, although wilful, has made a vow of obedience and in the play there are times when her independent spirit comes to the fore: her jesting with Iago, her insistence Othello speak to her about Cassio's demotion; but there are other times when she shows wifely obedience, especially when instructed to accompany him or go to bed.

Point 5: Emilia highlights there are very few differences between men and women. Even suggesting women have the same sexual appetites. She is disparaging of men for simply using women as *"food"*.

Point 6: She even suggests it is men's fault if women fail. If men are more intelligent, more capable, keepers of women, then if they don't live up to the role, instructing their womenfolk by example, then how is it women can be blamed if they fail? Surely it is due to the man's inability to lead?

<u>Point 7</u>: Her deduction of Iago's *"villainy"* at the end of the play shows how women can be as intelligent as men.

<u>Point 8</u>: Bianca is sorely abused by Cassio and Iago. Cassio sees her as merely a means of satisfying his bodily lust, not as a potential wife. He ridicules her adoration, finding her irksome. This is in contrast to Othello and Desdemona's mutual adoration.

Iago, calling Bianca, *"trash"*, accuses her of being involved in Roderigo's murder.

<u>Conclusion</u>: The women in *Othello* are either classified as wives or whores by the men. They are used and abused, expected to do their spousal duty, be a means of satiating men's lust and show obedience and subservience. Yet, Shakespeare shows women to be able to wield a power over men, be as intelligent, if not more so than them and dares suggest that if men do not set a good example, then surely women will fall.

Section 6.11: Plan for an essay on Imagery in *Othello*

(Please refer to the section on imagery for a more comprehensive essay.)

Introduction: Images are used to highlight themes and character traits. Major images in *Othello* are: sight and blindness, disease and corruption, food, natural images and references to the gods, heavens and hell and magic. Light and dark and clothing imagery depend on the production.

Point 1: The image of sight and blindness highlights the theme of prejudice, appearance versus reality and emotion versus reason.

Brabantio cannot see past Othello's *"sooty"* complexion, whereas the duke and Desdemona can. The duke sees him as a fine soldier; Desdemona, a worldly man.

Iago is deemed as *"honest"* by Othello, Cassio and Desdemona. They are blind to his evil as he puts on an appearance of a friend. Eventually Roderigo suspects the ancient has played false and Emilia deduces his *"villainy"*.

Othello's jealousy blinds him to Iago's evil. Desdemona too is blinded by love, not seeing her husband's jealousy. Roderigo is completely enamoured as well.

Ironically it is Iago who is not blind to the flaws of others and uses these to *"feed [his] revenge"*.

Point 2: Shakespeare uses sickness imagery to highlight the theme of love, jealousy and betrayal.

Roderigo is love-sick, Desdemona cured Othello's pains when she fell in love with him and the Moor goes *"mad"* when he suspects his wife's betrayal, believing his bed to be *"contaminated"*.

In contrast Iago's hatred for Othello is *"a poisonous mineral"* and he plans to make Othello literally sick with jealousy, pouring *"pestilence"* into his ear.

Othello notes Desdemona appears feverish when he has proof of her betrayal and Cassio, having been betrayed by Iago, is

"hurt past all surgery".

Point 3: The image of food emphasises the themes of emotion versus reason and love.

Iago comments jealousy eats away at a person's sanity and passion is all-consuming. He believes the ruination of Cassio and Othello will *"feed"* his revenge.

Cassio loses his reputation by allowing alcohol to stifle his reason.

Emilia views women as *"food"* to satisfy men's sexual *"appetites"*. The word *"sweet"* is used as a term of endearment.

Point 4: Iago uses natural imagery to consider predetermination versus freewill. Seeing men as *"gardeners"* Iago has the ability to shape the destinies of others. He cultivates *"syrups"* and *"poisons"* to assist him in his quest for *"revenge"*.

The love song *"Willow"* is representative of Emilia and Desdemona's demise.

Point 5: Heaven and hell equate with goodness and evil in the play. Desdemona is surrounded by heavenly imagery whereas Othello suffers the pains of hell as he discovers his wife's supposed betrayal.

Looking to the heavens for guidance and confirmation is done in times of adversity.

Iago is surrounded by devil and monster imagery, highlighting his *"villainy"* and bringing to the fore the appearance versus reality theme.

Jealousy is metaphorically compared with a feeding *"monster"* as is the sin of adultery.

Othello asks,

"Who can control his Fate?"

questioning do people have freedom of choice or are people's lives in the lap of the gods?

Point 6: The images of light and dark highlight good and evil. Murders carried out in the dark, Iago's soliloquies are often shrouded in darkness. There is also the symbolism of bringing the truth to light.

Point 7: The magic imagery stresses the theme of love. Othello is accused of using *"witchcraft"* to woo Desdemona, and the handkerchief he gives her is believed to have magical powers. The magic of love is highlighted when two people of different cultures and ethnicities fall in love.

Point 8: Clothing highlights the appearance versus reality theme. The characters in this play should be well dressed, but Roderigo's gentlemanly appearance belies a gullible fool, Othello a man turned mad by his jealousy and Iago, evil incarnate. Desdemona may be dressed in white signifying innocence and purity, but she has an independent spirit.

Conclusion: Shakespeare uses imagery to great effect in *Othello*. The images highlight themes and character traits, adding a further layer of interest to the play.

Section 6.12: Plan for an essay on

"Shakespeare's play demonstrates the weakness of human judgement." Discuss this statement supporting your answer with the aid of suitable reference to the text.

<u>Introduction</u>: Much of the drama relies on the characters being poor judges of their fellow men and women. Shakespeare, via clothing and sight and blindness imagery, warns not to judge a person by their appearance, nor by what they hear. Ironically it is Iago who can see his fellow characters for what they are, then uses their flaws to machinate his evil plans.

<u>Point 1</u>: Roderigo is a poor judge of character not realising until the very end of the play that Iago used him for *"sport"* and *"profit"*.

His love for Desdemona blinds him to the fact she is besotted with the Moor and he only wants to hear Iago's words of encouragement to pursue his suit. Iago abuses Roderigo's desire for his own gain, resulting in the gentleman's ruin and demise.

<u>Point 2</u>: Love too blinds Desdemona to the Moor's flaw of jealousy. She misjudges Othello, not knowing his jealous nature will enrage him to the point of wanting to kill her.

<u>Point 3</u>: Othello misjudges Iago believing him *"honest"* thereby has no doubts when his ancient produces *"proof"* of Desdemona's supposed adultery and of Cassio's betrayal. He believes everything Iago says, thus Iago can work his *"poison"*.

The Moor misjudges Emilia, not believing her when she tells him his wife has been *"honest"* and faithful.

Tragically, he misjudges Desdemona, not believing her when she tells him she is *"your true and loyal wife"*.

<u>Point 3</u>: Cassio too shows weak judgement, trusting Iago and thinking him *"honest"*. He allows the ancient to ply him with drink and has no idea he is being duped. Furthermore, he does as Iago instructs and asks for Desdemona to speak favourably of him to her husband.

<u>Point 4</u>: Emilia is slow to realise the *"villainy"* of her husband, not knowing what he will do with the handkerchief, but in the final scene deduces Iago's involvement in the death of Desdemona. Like others she has shown weak judgement of her husband, yet she has a shrewd understanding of men, maltreating women to satiate their lustful *"appetites"*.

<u>Point 5</u>: Lodovico misjudges Iago and the Moor. When he sees Othello strike his wife, he is appalled, but even more so when he reads the letters written by Roderigo proving Iago's guilt.

<u>Point 6</u>: Bianca misjudges Cassio's feelings for her, unaware of his disdain.

<u>Point 7</u>: The audience first hears of Othello via derogatory animal imagery. Would the audience misjudge Othello until he appears in fine clothes and speaks eloquently? Would their prejudice knowing he is a Moor, who has married a white Venetian, cause them to misjudge him?

Would the audience show weakness of judgement if they did not know of Iago's machinations via his asides and soliloquies? Ironically Iago knows his appearance belies a very evil reality.

<u>Conclusion</u>: Roderigo, Cassio and Othello show weakness of judgement not seeing Iago's true self. Love and prejudice blinds the characters and even though all are well-dressed, their clothes hide their true selves. Shakespeare even dupes the audience into initially believing Othello to be a

"ram", a *"Barbary horse"*, ensuring viewers will empathise with those who show lack of judgement on stage.

Section 6.13: Plan for an essay on "Othello is a character with whom the audience can sympathise." Discuss with reference to and quotation from the play.

Introduction: Othello is a victim of the machinations of a master deceiver, Iago, whose desire for vengeance ensures Othello's downfall. Can an audience sympathise with Othello for being a victim of prejudice, for being blinded and deluded by love, and for being somewhat gullible? Possibly cannot sympathise with a man who becomes *"mad"* with jealousy, who strikes his wife and commits uxoricide. His suicide provokes sympathy, but can be seen as a just punishment for his flaws.

Point 1: Othello is a victim of prejudice voiced mainly by Brabantio but echoed by Iago. Sympathise with him as the Moor is prejudged and derided by others as a *"black ram"*, suggesting lasciviousness. He is a nobleman in the eyes of his people and capable of commanding a fleet to victory against the formidable Turks. His downfall is more poignant because of his victory.

Point 2: Desdemona sees beyond Othello's skin colour and an audience can sympathise with Othello falling in love with such a pure, chaste noblewoman. However, his love for her blinds him to the machinations of Iago and inspires the jealousy that blinds his reason.

Point 3: Iago is a master of deception and thus to a certain extent I can sympathise with Othello's belief that Iago is *"honest"*. Othello is fooled by an intelligent man, who orchestrates *"a web"* of deceit ensuring he becomes insanely jealous. One can pity Othello when he falls *"into an epilepsy"*, especially when Iago is seen to be relishing the Moor's pain.

Point 4: Yet is Othello's obsessive jealousy, his hamartia, with which I cannot sympathise. He looks for *"proof"* of Desdemona's infidelity but never faces her directly with the charge. The *"green ey'd monster"* overcomes Othello's reasoning and I cannot sympathise with a man who resorts to striking his wife. Othello's base behaviour in Cyprus reflects the barbarism expected by the Turks.

Point 5: Othello is

> *"led by the nose as asses are"*

by Iago, who ensures Cassio's demotion; deceives Othello using the handkerchief and ensures he misinterprets a conversation between himself and Cassio, whereby the Moor believes Desdemona to be unfaithful (whereas Cassio is discussing Bianca). Othello does not rationalise Desdemona's actions, but sees what he is led to believe. One can sympathise with Othello having been betrayed by a man he thought to be a friend.

Point 6: Cannot sympathise with Othello's decision to see Desdemona punished. He acts as judge, jury and executioner damning her to hell, but then relenting by ensuring she has *"prayed tonight"* before suffocating her. His decision to take his own life reflects his impulsiveness, and can sympathise with him as he condemns himself to *"hell fire"* by committing suicide. However, his decision to take his own life negates the need to try him for uxoricide.

Conclusion: Othello is a man who provokes sympathy and yet, at times, does not deserve any pity. I can sympathise with him as a victim of prejudice, as a victim of Iago's machinations and for his jealousy leading to madness. I cannot sympathise with his violence, his complete blindness to Iago and his avoidance of discussing his suspicions with his wife. He did

> *"the state some service"*

but

> *"loved not wisely but too well".*

His final speech before his demise is a plea from his heart to be remembered for his better judgements rather than his flaws.

Section 6.14: Plan for an essay on Dramatic Scene(s) in *Othello*

<u>Introduction</u>: *Othello* is a tragedy and thus has to have the two major elements of Shakespearean theatre: fear and pity. All good drama requires tension or suspense, with the added bonus of sex and violence.

These elements can be found in the final scene.

<u>Point 1</u>: The audience fears for Desdemona when Othello's threatens to kill her. Furthermore fear is emoted when Iago attacks Emilia. Note the sexuality of the scene as it takes place in the intimacy of the bedroom and the light and dark imagery, Othello carrying a candle to shine a light on Desdemona's supposed betrayal.

<u>Point 2</u>: The audience pity the two women who are innocent victims. (Although Emilia's role can be questioned. Depending on her involvement, does she deserve to die?) Heaven and hell and monster imagery highlights Iago's treachery.

<u>Point 3</u>: Violence is swift and fatal. The deaths of Desdemona and Emilia (uxoricide) are quickly followed by the death of Othello (via suicide) and news of Roderigo's demise.

<u>Point 4</u>: Tension is created as the audience question the fate of the murderers. Othello chooses his own fate, (suicide), but Iago's punishment is left open. Even at very end of the play the audience leaves the theatre still questioning what befalls Iago. (In Orson Welles' production, Iago is hoisted in a cage high up on the castle walls, left alive to be eaten by the crows.)

<u>Point 5</u>. The play concludes with the open question of what will Cassio do? Does Othello deserve a state funeral as he has done the *"state some service"*? Audience experiences fear of Othello going to hell as he has sinned against God.

Does the audience have any pity for Othello or Iago? Heaven and hell imagery aid the fear factor.

Another dramatic scene is Act IV Scene I when Othello overhears a conversation between Cassio and Iago, believing they are speaking of Desdemona.

<u>Point 1</u>: The tension mounts as Iago's plan to turn Othello *"mad"* works.

<u>Point 2</u>: Fear factor is created as Iago sounds so sincere. Thanks to the soliloquy (aside) the audience are aware of Iago's machinations and Cassio's innocence. Wonderful use of dramatic irony.

<u>Point 3</u>: Light and dark imagery is employed as Othello is hidden and Cassio is metaphorically in the dark. Darkness highlights Iago's *"villainy"*. In a moment of truth Iago actually admits

"I am a very villain"!

<u>Point 4</u>: Sexuality is brought to the fore. Cassio's dalliance with Bianca is merely for his pleasure and he laughs about the relationship. Thereby pity for women is evoked as Cassio's dismissal of Bianca is hurtful.

"Marry her ... bear some charity to my wit".

The words *"She haunts me"* suggests she is irksome and a weak willed woman.

<u>Point 5</u>. Violence that ensues is emotional. Othello rages about what he will do to Desdemona.

"I will chop her into messes...foul".

Sickness imagery abounds. She has *"contaminated"* the marital bed.

Iago suggests Othello *"strangle her"*.

Point 6: Thus the tension mounts. Will Othello kill his wife? Will he kill his *"lieutenant"*? Othello asks Iago,

"How shall I kill him?"

and Iago volunteers to kill Cassio, saying,

"Let me be his undertaker".

Darkness and light imagery conclude this scene with Othello and Iago arranging to meet once again at *"midnight"*. (The witching hour!)

Conclusion: The scenes contain all the elements of good drama, employing imagery to highlight characters and themes and dramatic irony to create tension. The violence leads to the audience experiencing both fear and pity.

Section 6.15: Plan for an essay on
"Iago is an insidious villain with whom the audience has no sympathy." Discuss with reference to and quotation from the play.

Introduction: Iago is seen by many as an odious *"demi-devil"*, and even admits to be a *"villain"*. His evil *"web"* of deceit results in tragedy, but I would argue there are a few times in the play when I can sympathise with Othello's ancient, but not condone his actions.

Point 1: His treatment of Roderigo is abhorrent. He uses the gentleman for *"profit"* and for *"sport"*. To *"diet his revenge"* he spins his *"web"* of lies and manipulation to bring about the ruin of Cassio and Othello.
BUT
I can sympathise somewhat as Iago was overlooked for promotion. Cassio is a younger man and less experienced.

Point 2: His abuse of women is odious. He treats his wife like *"food"*, demanding she do his bidding and steal the *"handkerchief"*. Furthermore, he thinks nothing of accusing Desdemona of adultery, knowing she is innocent.
BUT
Is Iago merely a product of the times when women were treated like second-class citizens? I can understand his contempt for women, but can I sympathise with it? In a very short scene Iago verbally spars with Desdemona, both showing their sense of humour and their ability to play on words. Here Iago shows a more human side, but I have to question whether this too is a pretence.

Point 3: Via his soliloquies the audience sees a more human side of Iago. He is a passionate, intelligent man but he puts his intelligence to evil rather than to the greater good.

Can I sympathise with his reasons for *"revenge"*? He believes Cassio and Othello have slept with his wife.

Point 4: Yet I cannot have sympathy for a man who shows no remorse and who looks to blame others for his crime. At the end of the play he refuses to speak, suggests Bianca is involved in Roderigo's death and kills his wife to stop her from deducing his *"villainy"*.

BUT

I am not an advocate of *"torture"* and see no point in torturing Iago considering there is ample proof of his crimes. I hope Cassio can find it in his heart to swiftly punish the man, for whom ultimately I have little sympathy.

Section 6.16: Plan for an essay on
Shakespeare is a poet and a playwright of great renown. How is this proved in the play *Othello*?

Introduction: Shakespeare uses many devices in his work, which have been emulated by others. He uses literary devices, stage devices and instils pity and fear into his audience. He uses imagery and irony to highlight themes and characters, create atmosphere and add tension. (Please refer to previous notes to assist in this essay).

Point 1: Use of literary devices adds a poetic quality to the play, emphasising character traits, thoughts, actions and themes. Give examples.

Point 2: Use of rhyme to highlight erudition and the emotion versus reason theme in the play. Give examples

Point 3: As a playwright Shakespeare brings his play vividly to life. Consider the following:
contrasting characters,
action sequences
music
costume design
fear and pity

Point 4: As a writer Shakespeare uses imagery to highlight themes and issues. Repetition of imagery ensures the themes and issues are memorable as well as adding variety to the play.

Point 5: Irony aids tension and makes the play more interesting and as entertaining on subsequent viewings. Knowing Iago's plans heightens the drama.

Point 6: Use of contrast of settings ensures the audience are captivated by the locales and highlights the disparate goings on within Venice and Cyprus, adding to the entertainment value of the play.

<u>Conclusion</u>: Shakespeare's mastery of language is shown in his repeated images conveying fully the tragedy of *Othello*. He makes full use of stage devices available to him and these are also seen in film today. His repeated imagery ensures themes and issues are fully portrayed and the inclusion of prophecy makes the play rewarding on subsequent viewings. Above all Shakespeare's work is left open to interpretation, ensuring productions are varied and therefore entertaining, proving Shakespeare is a poet and playwright of great renown.

Further Books in this Series

Assisting Examination Candidates in The Study of King Lear.

Assisting Examination Candidates in The Study of Hamlet.

Look out for further books in this series available in the coming months.

Other Titles by A E Chambers

Fiction:

Reprehensible

Change of Plans

Take Ten: A Collection of Short Stories

Puzzling It Out

Fathom It Out

An Easter Gift

Make All The Difference

Made in the USA
San Bernardino, CA
18 July 2019